DOG

STORIES OF DOG OWNERSHIP

JULIAN VICTORIA

BOOKS

In memory of Maisie, who inspired our book cover illustration. Maisie was a rescue puppy originally found alongside a Texas road. She became Rob Wilson's muse over the years as they moved to New York City. Her magic continues to inspire and delight in many of Rob's drawings.

Julian Victoria
Creative Director and Design

Chelsea Joy Arganbright
Writer

Jake Tyas
Rob Wilson
Illustrations

Joshua Lawrence
Luciano R. Munhoz
Landon Speers
Julian Victoria
Photography

Ellie Whitlock
Production Assistant

Eve Marleau
Commissioning Editor

Gillian Haslam
Copy Editor

Lisa Fiske
Production Controller

Published in 2022 by Hardie Grant Books,
an imprint of Hardie Grant Publishing

Hardie Grant Books (London)
5th & 6th Floors
52–54 Southwark Street
London SE1 1UN

Hardie Grant Books (Melbourne)
Building 1, 658 Church Street
Richmond, Victoria 3121

hardiegrantbooks.com

British Library Cataloguing-in-Publication Data. A catalogue record for this book is available from the British Library.

ISBN: 978-1-78488-441-3

Colour reproduction by p2d. Printed in China by Leo Paper Products Ltd.

MIX
Paper from
responsible sources
FSC™ C020056
FSC
www.fsc.org

CONTENTS

14

The Airedale Terrier

Dries Van Noten + Scott

30

The Border Terrier

Sarah Bell + Raph

44

The Kerry Blue Terrier

Anna Barnett + Ted

60

The Chihuahua

Mexico

78

The English Bulldog

Carlo Lanzini + Beppe & Angelina

94

The French Bulldog

Russell Tovey + Rocky

108

The Labrador

Alistair Petrie + Mara & Zooey

124

The Mixed Breed

Remi Wolf + Juno

138

The Toy Poodle

Katy and Saeed Al-Rubeyi + Party

156

The Pug

Matthew Malin and Andrew Goetz + Mr Greenberg

174

The Shiba Inu

Japan

190

The Whippet

Rosie Birkett + Cyril

INTRODUCTION

An unparalleled sense of joy lifts the soul the moment the front door opens to a feverishly swaying tail and the clamour of paws dancing upon the floor. Only dog owners can experience this simple yet inimitable thrill. Memories of the day's stressors simply dissipate when greeted by a companion whose primary purpose is to provide unconditional affection for its owner. A canine's innocent zeal for life is contagious and as dog owner Alistair Petrie says, 'The instant you look at a dog, your mind cannot think of anything else.' Owning a dog alters the entire framework of one's life. The journey of dog ownership is a deeply personal experience and one which can only be adequately conveyed through the medium of intimate storytelling. This book provides accounts of the all-encompassing impact canines have on our lives, as told by inspirational dog owners in the midst of their own particular journeys.

Based on the London publication DOG Magazine, this book is a celebration of the relationship we have with our beloved canines. The narratives are shared by a range of creatives in various vocations who let us in on their everyday lives, proffering advice from the diverse knowledge acquired during their experiences as dog owners. Not only are the individuals honest and raw in communicating their anecdotes but they do so in a way we can all garner inspiration from. No matter the industry or echelon, once stripped down, the conversations all comprise a common undercurrent: a deep-seated love and appreciation for dogs. It's this very same theme which connects us to one another as a community of dog owners, something which might be unfathomable for non-dog owners to comprehend. 'Rocky is the best thing that has ever happened to me,' remarks Russell Tovey, actor and art curator, who is as passionate about his French Bulldog as he is about his multifaceted career endeavours.

However, this guide is not intended as a sugar-coated anthology. It reveals the intricacies of what it really means to be a dog owner, with all the jubilation and hardships therein. While Matthew and Andrew of Malin + Goetz recollect their rescue Pug Mr Greenberg's early separation issues each time they departed their New York residence, Katy and Saeed – founders of Story MFG – divulge their exhaustion from attempting to rehabilitate a Poodle from its traumatised past. Developing any relationship is never a black and white experience, and this is the very same for the relationships with the dogs we choose to bring into our lives. There is a beauty in standing strong when things might not go as planned, and the subsequent rewards of enjoying a happy, healthy dog are absolutely invaluable. To foster a healthily-integrated relationship such as the one Dries Van Noten has with his Airedale, Harry, is an aspiration for us all.

Even if the scene of your everyday life differs greatly from the prominent, fascinating lives of the dog owners featured here, you can still extract essential pieces of advice from their stories. The functional tips and tricks span what to look for when researching breeders, breed-specific health concerns to keep in mind and lifestyle considerations when incorporating a new dog into the home. This guide will assist readers to make informed decisions on the most suitable breed for their circumstances and help current dog owners to understand how they might be able to further enrich the relationship they have with their pet. It covers everything from elation to grief and trepidation to chagrin and the small, simple moments that make it all worthwhile. It can also simply act as a reminder to see the humour when your dog has gotten into mischief again.

THE
AIREDALE TERRIER

Quintessentially English, the Airedale's prominent stature was born from humble roots. A working-class dog, the Airedale was strategically teamed up with ferrets on rat hunts whereby the ferret would flush the rat out of its burrow and the Airedale would then attend to its capture. This was the 1800s and at the time, the Aire River Valley in Yorkshire was in need of not only a decent rat-catcher but a multipurpose breed which could also retrieve, guard and even drive cattle home. News of the Airedale's capabilities spread across Europe, and from across the continent the Germans recognised this tenacity and spirit and imported the breed to harness its dynamic abilities as police and later military dogs during World War I. Working alongside German Shepherds, Rottweilers and Dobermann Pinschers, these heroic dogs were employed to carry ammunition, track wounded soldiers in the battlefield, alert soldiers of explosives and deliver critical messages. The skilful Airedale even learnt to don a gasmask while carrying out duties on the frontlines. Midway through the war, the British discovered the resource which had hitherto been right under their noses and utilised the dogs in World War II with the aid of Colonel Edwin Richardson's British War Dog School. The Airedale's efforts are an indelible part of British history which translated into its soaring post-war popularity. Since then, the Airedale has become the ideal family dog for those looking for a sturdy and outgoing breed to integrate into their energetic lifestyle.

DRIES VAN NOTEN
+ SCOTT

Belgian fashion designer mogul Dries van Noten knows exactly how to harness historical authenticity in his designs whilst integrating a modern flair. His penchant for fully appreciating a story can easily be surmised by understanding his love affair with his own Airedale, Scott. Van Noten, a pure Anglophile, is not only acutely aware of the breed's British wartime history but sees the Airedale as the true king of the terriers, partly due to their sheer gumption cultivated during their development. He remarks, 'Airedales had to undergo being fitted into peculiar gas masks and were adept at transporting food and medicine to soldiers in need on the battlefield.' Patrick Vangheluwe, Van Noten's business and life partner, proffers: 'Little do people know, Airedales were used in the same way as police dogs in Germany. They're incredibly talented.' The men also admire the Airedale's classic element and mental strength. 'They are positively an all-in-one dog. While being exceptionally wilful, it's difficult to break their character. That's what we appreciate most about the breed.' Vangheluwe suggests, 'It's like when a child draws a dog on a piece of paper, it looks just like an Airedale. They are simply the perfect dog.'

One can sense traces of Scott's notable ancestors in his bold temperament. Van Noten affirms, 'He has such a strong personality; though he is quite clumsy, he is definitely not a Labrador. The Airedale bloodline is incredibly strong.' One crucial aspect of the Airedale breed is their propensity to create a challenge for their owner. He explains, 'One must be open to raising a characteristically insubordinate dog when opting for an Airedale. I can perfectly imagine some people could feel an Airedale's personality is much too intense for them. While some breeds are underneath the human in the hierarchy, an Airedale insists on perpetually existing on the same level.' His calm, slightly methodical demeanour comes across, 'The most critical thing is for the Airedale and human to learn to respect and appreciate one other.' Vangheluwe's intuitive wisdom arises, 'You can always read how Airedales think – they are profoundly readable.'

Growing up, both Van Noten and Vangheluwe's families raised Airedales. On Van Noten's side, this was alongside a Collie, Irish Setter, Flemish Sheepdog and Cocker Spaniel. As for Vangheluwe, his family raised German Shepherds, Bouviers and Rottweilers along with an Airedale. Despite the plethora of breeds experienced by the two men, the Airedale was always the indisputable choice. Once Van Noten ventured to Antwerp to study fashion, he of course had little time to own pets. However, when he and Vangheluwe moved in together, they adopted a cat which thrived for an exceptionally healthy 16 years. They explain how even though they weren't cat-people, they ironically owned a cat for such a long period and this further cultivated their entrenched values around pet ownership. Once the cat passed away, the men quickly realised how entirely empty the house felt. This was the spark to seeking out their first beloved Airedale, Harry.

Harry's temperament was quite juxtaposed with Scott's, though equally as strong. Van Noten remarks, 'They are two completely different dogs. Both strong in pride and naughty in character. We named Harry after Prince Harry –English, red-haired and a bit naughty. With Harry you had to earn his love by appealing to him. He was not nearly as social as Scott and simply loved sitting outside, enjoying the world on his own. He was a typical loner while Scott is quite the opposite: exceptionally generous with his love.' Though Harry had to be given an ample amount of attention to deem his owners worthy of his affection, when it came to small children it was an entirely different story. Harry allowed them to parade him around endlessly and it is very much the same with Scott – transforming into the perfect dog on the lead. Meanwhile, when it comes to walking with his owners, Scott knows he can get away with being naughty the moment the lead is clipped on. Airedales' intelligence allows them to take liberties as they please.

In addition to Scott's notoriously larrikin ways, he maintains various other quirks which only add to his appeal. While Harry could sleep away the evening while his owners enjoyed the opera or theatre, Scott experiences particular challenges on his own. This is an aspect of Scott the pair have had to adapt their lives and schedules to. Vangheluwe chortles, 'When we arrive home, it always feels as though it has been days since Scott has seen us – perhaps he has a very short memory.' Scott's main joy is for everyone in the household to be close together: 'The more people who are together, including the housekeeper and our sister-in-law, the happier he is. If everyone is nearby, he will lay directly in the doorway so he can keep an eye on who is coming and going.' Scott is indeed a sensitive soul.

Van Noten and Vangheluwe own a holiday home in an Italian seaside village which, under normal circumstances, they frequent over the summer, in addition to stints in Paris, London, New York and the Far East. Though they typically leave Scott with their sister-in-law while abroad, they once took Scott with them to Italy. However, as the locals frequently set fireworks off in the evenings, this did not sit well with him. Vangheluwe summarises, 'It seemed like the universe exploded for Scott – he stayed in the house for days just shaking.' Since then, they make it a rule to leave him in the care of trusted family members. Many dogs are understandably shaken by the overwhelming clatter of fireworks which is why it is particularly crucial to tune in with their sensitivities – and like Scott's owners, leave them in the trusted care of housesitters or family members instead of putting them through an experience which could prove traumatising for them.

The story of how Scott manifested into the lives of Van Noten and Vangheluwe is wholly endearing. When Harry sadly died in late 2019, they agreed to never again own a dog as in the end it brought too much suffering. Nonetheless, Harry's breeder phoned them only three weeks after learning of Harry's death to convince them otherwise. He explained how he had planned to use an Airedale named Spot as his sire, but found he lacked a single back tooth. This rendered him unsuitable for breeding, as is often the case when pedigree perfection is so esteemed. Fortunately, however, Airedales are in high demand and the breeder asserted that Spot would have quickly been snapped up in only a day. Thus, he reached out to the duo to see if they would like to take him. Van Noten recalls, 'At first, we were completely against the idea.' The breeder sent photos to them and of course the men could not resist scheduling a booking to see him. In preparation for the visit, they placed a blanket on the back seat of their car – just in case. The rest is history as both Van Noten and Vangheluwe immediately fell in love with Spot – who they renamed Scott as it was close enough to his given name and kept with the British theme, harking back to a tasteful moniker like F. Scott Fitzgerald. Though they felt a certain nervousness that a dog of seven months would prove difficult to raise, the breeder insisted he would develop a great temperament.

As the breeder was incredibly reputable and only bred on a few occasions each year, Van Noten knew he could trust his word which has proven to be nothing but true.

Scott's youthfulness keeps the pair on their toes. 'He reminds us of an eternal puppy as he errs on the uncoordinated side. He really behaves like a one-year-old dog even though he's getting on to three years now. He often runs into trees and bumps into things – it's quite charming, but he is definitely not the most artful Airedale.' Scott's job seems to be keeping his owners endlessly entertained. 'He will often see a rabbit and run like crazy, however the rabbit is already long gone! He once caught a rabbit and was so surprised when it squeaked, Scott dropped it immediately as he felt he had done something wrong. He was used to having stuffed animals which didn't emit a noise and so was not expecting a squeak from this one.'

Scott also enjoys spending his time hurtling after pheasants and deer. Vangheluwe elaborates, 'He is like a car in the fifth gear when he spots a deer; he is fixated. Scott's hunting instinct is much more developed than Harry's was. Scott even broke his leash on one occasion – he is incredibly strong. Luckily, the deer always run faster than him.' Scott also gets a thrill out of teasing the geese who will be on one side of the pond and then dart to the other side upon spotting him. He and the geese end up running in circles. 'Eventually Scott wins as they'll fly away, resulting in Scott becoming quite happy with his accomplishment. He'll look to Patrick and I for acknowledgement.'

Scott's temperament has most definitely been moulded by the Covid-era. Van Noten suggests he is not quite as educated as he should be due to the past two years of government regulations: 'Scott is just a spoiled rebel because he has had all of our time and attention during the lockdowns.' Van Noten proffers advice to dog owners: 'Once schedules return to normal, it's about being responsible and balancing dog ownership duties with personal and professional responsibilities.' It is not uncommon for dogs to suffer separation anxiety after they have experienced prolonged periods with their owners. It requires a gentle and conscientious approach.

As dog-oriented as the pair are, they admit the culture of dog ownership is not as entrenched in Belgium as it is in England. Van Noten explains, 'There is a different mentality around dogs, it's not like in Britain. Pride around dog ownership is part of English rather than Belgian culture. Luckily, many of our neighbours own dogs and when we venture out for a wander around, there are typically a number of other dogs around for Scott to sniff.' Vangheluwe explicates, 'When a person owns a dog, they always having an immediate connection with others.' Van Noten chimes in, 'Being a dog-person feels similar to garden-oriented people: as Patrick says, there's always a common connection which you may not have had otherwise.'

When it comes to Van Noten's life in the fashion world, Scott is at the ready to step in as a model. Often when a fashion shoot takes place in the office, Scott quickly becomes one of the models and never seems to mind. The men laugh, 'Scott definitely enjoys it much more than Harry did. If Scott sees a photographer and white background, he sits patiently waiting as if to say, "When will it be my turn for a photo?"' Scott endlessly brings positive energy and jubilance into the both the office and household. Van Noten illuminates, 'Scott calms and soothes me, brings me into balance. He proves particularly helpful during difficult fittings; he's like a living stress ball. When things become too tense at work, we will have a cuddle or head out for a walk.' Van Noten divulges how he does not know how they would have survived the lockdowns without Scott: 'The idea of Patrick and me together for so many months without a dog is difficult to comprehend.' He light-heartedly offers how if he and Vangheluwe are not in the mood to speak with one another, they can always defer to Scott as he won't talk back or gossip to others. 'Owning a dog gives us a reason to do certain things we wouldn't otherwise do and provides a subject to talk about. He adds meaning to our lives.'

THE
BORDER TERRIER

Meandering through any classical art museum, one can easily catch sight of the sturdy Border Terrier featured within an array of English hunting paintings. One of the oldest terrier breeds in the country, its popularity has reigned for centuries. Many well-renowned Brits have personally selected this longstanding breed as their companion, which hints at both cultural tribute and recognition of their reliable natures. Though developed for hunting utility in the 1700s, using its fearless prowess to capture small animals proving bothersome to hardworking farmers, the Border Terrier remained unrecognised by the UK Kennel Club until 1920. Its unique double coat, comprising a soft underside and weather-resistant sheath, is as beneficial today on rainy day rambles as it was 300 years ago while rummaging through burrows for their masters' bounty. Its breeding heritage has seen a reinvigorated appreciation as it has passed on an amalgamation of innate intelligence and strong work ethic, rendering the breed relatively easy to train. It is for this reason that Border Terriers are often chosen to be utilised in movies as their willingness to please and adaptability is of particular advantage on set. While dog owners often voice their displeasure at the brevity of canine life, Border Terriers provide their owners with lasting joy as their lifespans usually range from twelve to fifteen years. As affectionate as they are industrious, the Border Terrier proves a solid, good-natured pet for the home.

SARAH BELL
+ RAPH

In this current generation, an air of entrepreneurialism sweeps through the culture as if innately present within each individual. This necessitates both an adaptability and an adeptness for dexterously balancing multiple pursuits. For Sarah Bell, this subtle art has become second nature as she sustains a thriving career, a growing family and her role as a dedicated dog owner to a spunky Border Terrier named Raph. Bell, founder of eco-friendly luxury candle brand Evermore, has devoted her life to scents and revels in the way they benefit the emotional states of her customers. She also has an awareness of the impact of fragrance on canine wellbeing as she utilises body sprays which calm the particularly lively Raph. In this way, she integrates her perfumery work into all aspects of her life, adding to the wellbeing of her customers and family alike through sheer sensory experience.

Eight years ago, Bell and her husband embarked on an adventurous road trip through Spain. As all the best ideas come from being on the road, the topic of baby names popped up, which prompted her husband to admit he always dreamt of naming his future son Raphael. Bell did not share the same eagerness for the name, but as a compromise she suggested if they ever acquired a dog, he could name it Raphael. It just so happened shortly after returning from the holiday they were enjoying a drink at a pub when they noticed a sign displaying the words 'Border Terrier Puppies for Sale'. The couple immediately drove to the farm in Yorkshire and upon arriving, only a single male remained amongst three females. Already set on a male due to the particularly affectionate nature male dogs tend to embody, the circumstance was meant to be. As promised, they named him Raphael – Raph, for short.

Back in the 18th century, across the hillsides running along the English-Scottish border, shepherds and farmers were faced with a cunning threat to their flocks. Hill foxes proved a nuisance for generations, prompting the breeding of a strategically engineered canine small enough to fit into fox dens with legs long enough to keep up with their masters on horseback, as well as commonly used Foxhounds. The Border Terrier's personality is as dynamic as its physical abilities as it is known to be a determined, spirited, family-oriented breed, demanding only low-maintenance upkeep. Their wiry coat is also entirely weatherproof, protecting them from the elements while their work-oriented nature indicates ensures an ease of training. It is for this reason that over the years, their popularity has extended from the fields to family homes throughout Britain.

Prior to witnessing the fateful 'For Sale' sign, Bell dug into extensive research for the exact type of dog that would fit in with her and her husband's active lifestyle. They did not want a dog too small or large and one which was fun, friendly and especially good with children. The Border Terrier breed fully fitted the bill. Though Border Terriers are characteristically social with other dogs, Bell explains, 'As Raph has always spent so much time with us without ever truly being on his own, he seems not to care about other dogs. He simply loves people.' When describing his temperament, Bell says he is a quintessential Border Terrier – with a nuanced and multi-layered streak. 'He has so much personality and we can always tell what mood he's in. Since maturing, he has become even more affectionate; when he was younger, he was often busy being curious and on the move.' Bell explains Raph is truly happiest when outside in the elements, suiting them perfectly as her husband is quite the outdoors enthusiast so he ensures they always have ample time for the stimulation of nature.

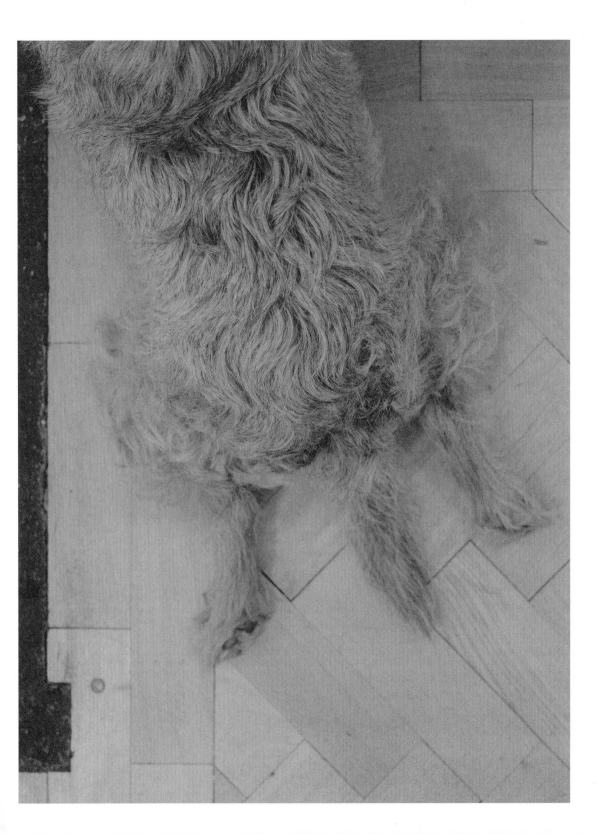

While enjoying an active lifestyle, Raph does not hold back on indulging. Bell chortles, 'Raph is the greediest dog in the world – we call him a "doggy dustbin". Besides bananas and prawns, he is deeply food motivated so we must be careful with portion control.' Bell explains Raph is quite a large-sized border terrier and the vet currently advises he could afford to lose a couple of pounds in weight. His diet consists of Lily's Kitchen dry biscuits mixed with offerings from the personalised online delivery company Butternut Box, which allows him to have balanced nutrition. Bell says, 'The dog food takes up more space in the freezer than the human food!'

In terms of quality time, Raph has been blessed with consistent interaction in Bell's work studio. She says, 'We centre our entire schedule around Raph.' They say this will soon change as the couple are expecting a baby and since all attention has been on Raph thus far, they worry about him feeling left out. Though fantastic with children, they anticipate he might feel jealous at the beginning, but adapt over time once he realises the baby is part of the family. Bell explains, 'Before a friend of ours came home from the hospital with their newborn baby, they brought home blankets which had been placed on the baby so their dog could anticipate what was coming. We will be doing the same.' Walking a dog alongside a pushchair prior to the baby's birth so the dog becomes accustomed to the peculiar foreign object is useful training, as is giving a dog treats while feeding the baby so the dog associates calmness with feeding time. It goes without saying to reward a dog for gentle behaviour around the baby is key. Introducing a newborn into a family always requires adjustment from everyone and this goes for the dog as well.

An overarching aspect of Bell and her husband's life is travel. They own a VW campervan which Raph adores as he knows it means he can look forward to playing in the sea. However, Bell confesses, 'Logistics are a big part of what we did not anticipate when getting a dog.' During their last campervan holiday to Cornwall, they decided not to take Raph as it was much too hot for him. Bell admits this was a refreshing change as it did not require the necessity of organising stays and meals strictly at dog-friendly venues. When the couple went on their first holiday abroad after getting Raph, the concept of kennels did not sit well with them so they booked him into a farm retreat. However, it was quite unsuccessful as Raph did not appreciate the farm experience and from that time forward, they developed a heavily strategised routine whenever taking a holiday: transferring Raph up to Bell's parents' home in Nottingham from London or alternatively driving him up to Yorkshire. Then, post-holiday, they drive back to retrieve him.

Fortunately, UK-based websites such as PetsPyjamas, Dog Friendly Cottages and BringFido eliminate some barriers to sourcing quality accommodation accepting dogs. Platforms like these offer a host of options such as train travel, luxury stays and even pub rooms. In addition, the ability to travel abroad with a canine companion opens up by obtaining a European pet passport accompanied by up-to-date vaccinations, especially as Rail Europe and the high-speed train service RailJet permit dogs in most of the countries they operate in. Careful coordination is required, but it is worth it when an owner can enjoy sprinting through Switzerland's Gastlosen Trails or meandering around dog-friendly Paris with his canine companion by his or her side. Bell emphasises, 'When you have a pet, you are fully tied to that creature with all decisions coming back to it.' She recommends fully researching the breed and taking into consideration location and working life when choosing a pup. It was not until her husband transitioned to freelance work when they decided to get a dog, and with Bell working from her own candle-making studio, it simply gels. Soon, Raph will even get to enjoy the VW campervan again – this time with a plus one. Hopefully he proves to be just as adaptable as his owner.

THE
KERRY BLUE TERRIER

Like its fellow terriers, the Kerry Blue Terrier was developed as a keen working dog. However, long before its strategic breeding for use on the fields was recognised, came the peculiar legend of its origins. A fleet of ships from the Spanish Armada set sail from Lisbon in 1588, bound for England with the intention of dethroning Queen Elizabeth I. The cunning British forces were far too skilful and wreaked havoc on the Spanish ships in the Strait of Dover, forcing them to retreat and navigate north towards Scotland. Most of these ships were wrecked along Ireland's west coast, including one which saw its demise off the coast of Country Kerry. In this particular ship, the only surviving member happened to be a single blue canine. The legend goes that this blue dog's will to survive carried it to land where he quickly became the alpha dog in the area and was mated with the local Soft Coated Wheaten Terriers, eventually resulting in what is now known as the Kerry Blue Terrier. Though a fantastical tale, there may easily be truth to it as the genetics of the breed show Portuguese Water Dog. Fast forward a few hundred years and the Kerry Blue Terrier enters into the political realm in Ireland as Irish nationalist and Kerry Blue owner Michael Collins pushed for its recognition as Ireland's national breed. Through the centuries, this highly spirited breed has shown its gumption while maintaining its position as one of the more independent and challenging breeds for dog owners.

ANNA BARNETT
+ TED

One could say Ted is a spry soul. His pastimes include paddleboarding sojourns in Wales and running along Cornwall's tranquil beaches, and he can be found on speedboats during water-skiing holidays, enjoying the salt water dusting his ebony coat. Ted is a particularly dynamic Kerry Blue Terrier, owned by chic food writer and home chef Anna Barnett. Barnett is as exceptionally multifaceted as her canine companion: She not only writes a column in The Evening Standard but also hosts a highly rated podcast, The Filling, where she discusses all things culinary with celebrities. Media has been an integral part of Barnett's life as her portfolio includes working with MTV, Channel 4, Vogue and British fashion label House of Holland, amongst dalliances with blogging and writing cookbooks. It therefore makes complete sense for Barnett to have a dynamic dog like Ted sharing her illustrious life.

Lounging in the sun-splashed garden of her east London residence, Barnett illustrates Ted's distinctive personality: 'He's so characterful... I feel he's only one step away from talking to me at all times.' He also happens to be from a split-family, but not in the way one might assume. He came as part of the package with her previous housemates – he was the runt of the litter and they aptly named him due to his resemblance to a teddy bear. Barnett joined their household one year on and soon shared ownership. When she relocated just around the corner, dog-sharing between the two homes became the norm and now twelve years on, it's Ted's dynamic way of life. This unique arrangement with the housemates provides Ted with constant love and company, each delivering him unique experiences which he revels in. For Ted, this arrangement looks like two weeks spent adventuring in the countryside and by the sea, followed by two weeks of London downtime with Barnett as he partakes in her business activities as a trusted kitchenhand. As almost all the cooking, writing and podcasting work is done from home, this means Ted is with her all of the time.

The degree of effort Barnett and the housemates put into Ted's well-rounded lifestyle is exemplary of dog ownership. Prior to purchasing or adopting a dog, choosing a breed which can easily amalgamate into the individual or family's lifestyle is vital. It should then be established whether the household routine can be re-arranged to accommodate a canine companion. Barnett imparts, 'It is incredibly important to make sure the dog is well-socialised, stimulated and integrated into a routine, whatever that looks like for your family.' Many Londoners maintain a versatile lifestyle at an energy level similar to Barnett's, making her advice crucial for future dog owners. If an individual does not have the proper time to devote to bringing up a dog as Barnett has done, then it is a question of whether a dog is a suitable decision for the individual or family.

In line with the Kerry Blue Terrier's personality, their traditional grooming style is equally as distinguished. The Kerry Blue's wavy, wool-quality fur grows continuously, making professional grooming every six weeks essential, supplemented by weekly brushing and trims. Barnett explains if she were to leave Ted's fur to its own devices in wintertime, it would become matted and difficult to manage, hence the need for her to stay on top of his grooming ritual - which he doesn't mind as he's quite fond of water. Ted regularly sports a classic Kerry cut, though most recently he has been seen sporting a shorter clip. In the early twentieth century, when the Kerry Blue was primarily utilised as a field dog in Ireland, the body coat was kept long and mostly unclipped as a practical measure, providing enhanced protection, with the hair left falling over the eyes and chin to give the dog a wild aesthetic. This evolved into what is now known as the notably sophisticated Kerry Blue grooming style involving full yet shaped legs, a closely cut torso and the quintessential beard and fall – a statement to symbolise the breed's transition into city show rings from farm fields.

The fiercely intelligent Kerry Blue Terrier originates from the lush, rolling hills of County Kerry. Barnett jokes at the fact their current popularity tends to be limited to a very specific older, Irish and male demographic and the breed is otherwise not well known, even within the UK. Kerry Blues were bred to be a superlative working dog with a keen adeptness for tracking and hunting small game and birds, along with the added responsibility of cattle and sheep herding. From 1926, to win the esteemed title of Irish Show Champion, Kerry Blues had to first demonstrate an ability to hunt rabbits, rats and badgers – an inherited predilection which has been passed down over the years, though breeders often attempt to breed the prey drive out of the bloodlines. Barnett warns that this particular brand of Kerry Blue Terrier formidability should not be underestimated as this ingrained predisposition translates into a tendency to not mesh well with other dogs and an enjoyment of pursuing small animals for capture. Barnett expounds on the Kerry Blue's capability: 'There's a saying that if you put a Kerry in a barrel with a badger, the Kerry Blue will come out on top. It's still prevalent in their breed.'

Barnett portrays Ted as incredibly loyal and people-loving, while tending to avoid most other dogs. A couple of scraps have been experienced which have proven worrisome for Barnett, leading her to reconsider where and when she walks him. As dogs can detect chemicals released from their owner's anxiety, this can become a revolving cycle which makes a calm, assertive demeanour integral to the relationship between canine and owner. Barnett explains, 'Until you see it, you don't know that's going to be prevalent within your dog. You either really have to know your dog through and through or you must be mindful they are unpredictable and each have their own personality.' Many breeds are chosen solely for their appearance or trendiness without an understanding of the breeding history. Researching the reason for the breed's development and the way this lineage affects their temperament are the foundational steps to bringing a dog into the household. If a breed displays a certain tendency, the owner must not blame the breed but be mindful to not introduce them to situations which trigger their genetic disposition, adapting the household routine to suit the characteristics of the dog.

Raising a well-adjusted dog requires early socialisation and the demonstration of leadership. Dogs maintain the pack mentality of their wolf predecessors, so if the owner does step into the alpha role, the dog will assume this position. Barnett affirms, 'Dogs should look to the owner for protection.' When an individual asserts himself as the alpha, it becomes the impetus for the dog's trust and respect which are cornerstones of the symbiotic dog-owner relationship, benefitting both in the long run. Barnett highlights the responsibility of proper training which requires time and perseverance appropriate to the chosen breed. Investment in training also ensures the dog feels as settled and comfortable in the home as possible. Barnett illustrates Ted's separation anxiety as he was initially accustomed to constantly being around humans, so when the households separated this affected him even though he still received copious amounts of love and affection. It is for this reason she proffers the advice for owners to train their dogs to be left at home alone for regular amounts of time in order to inhibit likelihood of separation-induced behaviours.

At twelve years of age, Ted has proven to be a force of nature. Despite developing a rare form of cancer in his leg, he still is as boisterous and able-bodied as ever. Barnett and the housemates made the difficult decision not to amputate, which they feel would have severely decreased his quality of life and instead focus on making Ted's life as happy and comfortable as possible without fixating on negatives. The veterinarian originally gave Ted up to six months to live; however, a year and a half later he is still going strong, perhaps due to his wilful personality combined with the doting love and care from his families. Barnett's culinary skills have also enhanced his wellness, as he now receives a specialised low-carb, vegetable-rich diet targeted at cancer mitigation as part of his regime for leading a healthier life. He also still enjoys a peanut butter-filled Kong and the odd hard-boiled egg as a treat.

Despite the trials and tribulations, Ted remains Barnett's enduring cooking companion and no matter the recipe she busies herself with, he enjoys the view from his dog bed at the end of the kitchen island, all the while carrying on conversations as they do in their own special way.

In memory of Ted, who after leading a full and happy twelve years of life sadly passed away a few months after this interview. He has left a lasting imprint on Anna who is ever grateful for his loyal companionship.

THE
CHIHUAHUA

With a rich history dating back to the Mayan and Toltec periods, the often misunderstood Chihuahua, named after the Mexican state, houses a reservoir of complexity. Not having been discovered worldwide until the 1850s, the Chihuahua was traced to a lineage stemming from the Techichi – a longhaired, barkless dog which was slightly larger than the modern-day Chihuahua. The Toltecs, who reigned during the Mesoamerican period between 900–1168 AD, specifically bred the Techichi as hunting and companion dogs. These dogs were considered to have supernatural gifts and were often buried with their owners so they could accompany them into the underworld. Ancient carvings and figures were found by explorers in the 1800s when uncovering the remains of the civilisation which show the Techichi appearing very much like the Chihuahua we know today, including the same apple and deer-head skull shapes. The genetics of the modern Chihuahua is approximately 70 per cent Techichi in origin and while the remainder is still unknown, researchers theorise it could consist of the Xoloitzcuintli or Maltese. In the late 1800s, merchants started to breed the Chihuahua for American tourists and by 1915, thirty Chihuahuas were registered by the American Kennel Club. However, as most dog breeds in the 1900s were developed for functional purposes, it was not until rapid urbanisation in the United States in the 1960s that dogs started to be considered for apartment living. As Chihuahuas generally embody a low-energy temperament, this combined with their miniature size makes the breed a sound selection for city dwellers looking for an adorable, transportable companion.

MEXICO

The people of Mexico are proud to recognise the Chihuahua as their canine ambassador. With a resurgence of popularity in recent times, the breed's age-old prominence has developed an exceptionally modern touch, and the reason is evident. The Chihuahua is an inherently dynamic breed which comes with its own set of customised attributes, in the realm of both aesthetics and personality. For those looking for ease of grooming, the short-haired Chihuahua is an obvious choice; however, as this variation is not well protected from the elements, a sweater would be in order during the winter months. The long-haired Chihuahua, also dubbed the rough-coated Chihuahua, is the alternative option but this demands a substantially rigorous grooming routine. The respective temperaments are the same, so it's simply a matter of the owner's coat preference and the time willing to be spent on trips to the groomer. In addition to the length of the coat, a multitude of colouring choices are available. Thirty coat colours are recognised by the American Kennel Club, in addition to a number of special markings including exotic choices such as Merle, Blue Mask and Black Sabling.

Akin to the Chihuahua's ancestors, when it comes to the curvature of the dog's profile, two genetic branches exist. The apple-head Chihuahua boasts a slightly bulbous head shape with a shorter snout, while the deer-head Chihuahua retains a relatively longer head and a straight snout. The single other perceivable distinction between the two versions is the fact deer-heads tend to have a larger frame than the petite apple-heads. And then there is yet another classification of the breed called the Teacup Chihuahua, which is undoubtedly the smallest breed in existence. However, with the numerous health issues arising due to improper breeding, the Teacup Chihuahua is generally not recommended by responsible professionals in the world of breeders.

When it comes to health generally, the Chihuahua is easily at the top of the list of canines least likely to have health worries. Often, they will exceed twenty years of age and achieve this goal with resilience and stamina. As Chihuahuas tend to shadow their owners no matter the activity, this can lead them to being prone to falls which means the owner must be diligent and keep an eye out for hazards. Teeth and bone issues can also become a concern, especially as the Chihuahua ages, though a well-rounded diet can mitigate these issues. The breed can also be susceptible to heart-related problems such as murmurs and circulatory issues, though this is a rarer occurrence. All things considered, the Chihuahua is effortlessly one of the healthiest breeds which treats its owner to decades of loyalty and companionship.

With their singularly characterful personalities, Chihuahuas have quite the reputation. Confidence, wilfulness and relentlessness are three terms which come to mind for many people when they first meet this small yet mighty breed. This of course can be a blessing and a curse all in one. Upon scoping out a significantly larger canine, they will typically assume they are of the same size and proceed to act accordingly. This misunderstanding of their physical stature can lead them to get themselves into trouble. However, with the Chihuahua's larger-than-life personality, it isn't uncommon to find that much larger dogs are afraid of the brave Chihuahua and back away when trouble stirs. When it comes to the human-dog connection, the Chihuahua adores being the centre of attention and typically builds a deep bond with a single individual in the household, which it then seemingly compares all others to. The breed is exceptionally willing to bestow affection onto its owner. As they are incredibly intelligent and eager for mental stimulation, training can come quite easily, although their stubbornness can at times put a spanner in the works. For this reason, agility training is a dynamic solution to instilling obedience while appealing to their active minds. When properly exercised and socialised, the Chihuahua is one of the most endearing breeds to raise.

Chihuahuas delight in donning a costume, which seems to fulfil their need to be in the spotlight. This is ideal as dog owners in Mexico, their country of origin, love to ensure their companions are properly adorned for any occasion. Each year on the feast day of Saint Anthony, animal lovers in Mexico dress their pets – from cockroaches to horses – in decorations of flowers, jewels and braids and accompany them to Mass. Saint Anthony the Abbot was said to be the great protector of the animals and on this day, the priest blesses each of the pets brought in on behalf of Saint Anthony. This tradition was started by Franciscan friars during the colonial era and it is a spectacle to behold. The owners of the animals ask for a blessing for their pet's health and following the service, a light-hearted competition is held where prizes are bestowed for the best-dressed pet. Perhaps this tradition is the reason why Mexicans revel in bedecking their dogs at any opportunity. In addition, the surge in Mexico's middle class has resulted in a burgeoning market for luxury items, including boutique canine attire. Meandering around Mexico's colourful urban street markets, it is not uncommon to see dog shampoos and fancy leashes on offer to cater to the dogs owned by the affluent members of society. As Mexicans adore their national breed, particular attention is paid to their dress sense and it's more likely to see a Chihuahua clothed than not. Parading the bustling streets of Mexico City in vibrant pink sweaters and furry coats, the country's exuberant temperament is truly embodied by none other than the sprightly Chihuahua.

THE
ENGLISH BULLDOG

Somewhat surprisingly, the gentle, charming English Bulldog has a murky past. The breed was developed from Mastiff origins in the 13th century and used to fight animals such as bears and bulls in a blood sport called bull-baiting, in which onlookers would place bets. Each aspect of the Bulldog's appearance was strategically designed for this sport. As the Bulldog was trained to bite at the nose of the beast, its snout was short so it could breathe properly and its lower jaw protruded outward to retain a better grip. The wrinkly, loose skin folds were seen to protect organs during a fight. As the Bulldog was bred to be low to the ground, this meant the bull would be less likely to reach it and throw it with its horns. Interestingly, although the Bulldog was fierce inside the ring, it was known to be particularly docile and reserved when not in the midst of provoked fighting. When bull-baiting was finally declared illegal in 1835, Bulldogs were carefully selected for breeding out aggressive tendencies and to allow the gentler aspects of the breed to remain. Up until World War I, the character John Bull was depicted alongside a Bulldog as a nationalist icon and to provoke wartime propaganda. Then, in World War II, the personification of England as a Bulldog was further instilled as Winston Churchill took on the nickname of the Bulldog which insinuated not only his physical features were reminiscent of this breed but also his character and directives during the war. In the past two centuries, the English Bulldog has been bred to become a patient, affectionate and even-keeled companion who can easily keep company with small children. The Bulldog's courageous, determined and independent temperament is a thoughtful reminder of British values to this day.

CARLO LANZINI
+ BEPPE & ANGELINA

In the gently rolling countryside of Puglia, on a ridge overlooking the Adriatic Sea lies Masseria Moroseta. A minimalist farmhouse set within an oasis of ancient olive groves, the masseria was jointly devised by founder Carlo Lanzini and architect Andrew Trotter utilising local materials and traditional building techniques. The property harks back to the original sixteenth-century masseria farm estates found exclusively in the Puglia region. Lanzini's passion for the land combined with an attention to forms and spaces has yielded an elegantly bucolic six-room retreat where he hosts international guests seeking tranquillity away from their everyday routines. Lanzini initially unveiled the property as a guesthouse, then placed his attention on the cultivation of the olives and biodynamic vegetables growing on the land. One year later, chef Giorgia Goggi joined Masseria Moroseta and guests were treated to Mediterranean-inspired dishes fused with international flair using the property's seasonal produce.

Lanzini, who grew up in the north of Italy in the countryside near Brescia, maintained a markedly different focus prior to settling in Puglia to construct his masseria. He bred French Bulldogs as a passion more than profession, which soon after pivoted to English Bulldogs once he bought his first, named Beppe, who is now a healthy twelve-year-old. Lanzini expresses, 'I became interested in English Bulldogs as they have more of a proper, strong dog character over French Bulldogs, who have beautiful temperaments but tend to be sillier which may not be fitting for every scenario.' Lanzini's time spent studying in London would make one think his sojourn inspired his fondness for the breed, however he suggests English Bulldogs currently seem to be even more popular in Italy than in Britain. Upon settling in Puglia, he realised there was plenty of space around and ultimately added two more English Bulldogs to the family: Angelina and Pablo.

The English Bulldog breed is described by Lanzini as the perfect option for the Masseria Moroseta property. He characterises them to be incredibly welcoming with a balanced character and displaying a certain playfulness, however without excessive boisterousness which could inhibit the guest experience. Lanzini asserts he would never choose any other breed as he adores the English Bulldog character: 'They're incredibly funny dogs and I just love their expressions.' Though his dogs have hectares of sprawling land to explore, Lanzini says, 'English Bulldogs are incredibly low energy, it is not in their blood to roam. They simply enjoy being near people, so they will play for a bit then become tired and require rest.' The property remains entirely unfenced, yet this is a non-issue as Beppe and Angelina are more than happy to stay close to the masseria. As a low-maintenance breed, their routine is left unstructured and they can choose to spend time in the farmhouse or stroll around the property between feeding and napping sessions. Lanzini says that at times he has seen an Instagram post from a guest the night before showcasing one of the dogs sleeping in their room. He comments, 'They have the most amazing life.'

Beppe and Angelina were bought from breeders in Bologna and Naples respectively. Lanzini describes Beppe as stubborn and moody; he enjoys keeping more to himself while Angelina at only one and a half years old is comparably playful and lively. As Beppe was Lanzini's first English Bulldog, bought at only two months old, he feels a special attachment to him. Beppe was alongside Lanzini as he embarked on the relocation to Puglia but he has also experienced the transition of the masseria from its foundations through to its current success. Lanzini observes, 'Sometimes Beppe will simply sit on the first floor of the masseria for hours, looking out to the sea as though he is the king of the castle.' Angelina, who with her abundance of wrinkles looked like a teddy bear upon arriving at the masseria, exhibits a youthful vitality which has brought a welcome energy to the property. Lanzini laughs, 'Angelina's passion is to chase lizards on the property but due to her size and plumpness, I don't think she will ever manage to catch one.'

While a comparatively undemanding breed in regards to temperament, English Bulldogs make up for it with their predisposition to particular health challenges. Pablo, Lanzini's second English Bulldog, arrived in Italy from a Spanish breeder who turned out not to have as much integrity as Lanzini expected. Pablo arrived at three months old with a bag of antibiotics in his crate intended to aid him with an undisclosed chronic respiratory issue, something Lanzini would spend a tremendous amount of energy and money on, including five operations spanning three years. Pablo passed away only last year due to his condition, which was so acute that surgery could not ultimately resolve it. Like other wrinkly, flat-nosed dogs, this susceptibility to breathing problems is all too common but not often addressed by many breeders. English Bulldogs with white coats like Beppe have further vulnerabilities as the lack of pigmentation increases their likelihood of skin cancer and allergies which Lanzini has been particularly careful about. To alleviate Beppe's allergies, he is fed only natural foods which, living at Masseria Moroseta, is not difficult to come by.

Lanzini sheds light on the disparity in dog culture between the north and south of Italy. In the north, Italians treat their dogs akin to British standards, i.e. cossetted like babies and at the least accepted as an integral part of the family. He has transposed this mentality into southern Italy which largely does not embrace dogs as pets but rather approaches them as a utility, whether through guarding homes or working the fields. Lanzini's approach to dog ownership captures the level of attention needed to raise a healthy, happy canine: 'The primary aspect people need to understand about English Bulldogs is the emphasis on health. They require weekly bathing due to their ample skin folds and an investment in quality, organic food is necessary due to their skin allergies. Even if the dog comes from a respected breeder, these health issues may still be embedded in the bloodline.' Lanzini bought Pablo from a breeder after seeing photos online and says he would never do this again as social media can too easily distort reality. His advice is to visit the dog and breeder in person before committing to buying.

Despite the trials in Lanzini's dog ownership journey, the quality of life which Beppe and Angelina enjoy at Masseria Moroseta is unsurpassed. Between the fresh air, unspoiled surroundings and simple sophistication, the masseria's restorative properties are as evident as they are unassuming. It is testament to the goodness in providing a dog, as well as people, with a free-range lifestyle – whether as a long-term abode to rest one's paws or for a taste of it during a couple's getaway. For those without the luxury of beginning anew in the countryside of Italy, a simple ramble in nature might suffice to satiate the thirst for revitalisation – or perhaps a pilgrimage to the masseria to call in on Beppe and Angelina.

THE
FRENCH BULLDOG

The French Bulldog's story begins not in France, but in England when it was known as the English Toy Bulldog. While the breed was utilised for its fighting proficiency, it was ranked by size and consequently placed into different categories – the smallest dubbed the English Toy Bulldog. Upon the eradication of bull-baiting, lacemakers in the mills of newly industrialising Nottingham took on the breed as a mascot of sorts – perhaps due to its small size and therefore humble feeding requirements. When machinery overtook the lacemakers' vocations during the Industrial Revolution, many of these skilled women relocated to France where their talents were still prized, taking with them their English Toy Bulldogs. It was there the breed was bestowed with its modern name: Bouledogue Français. Parisian ladies of the night were notorious for toting the characterful French Bulldogs around their brothels, while other working-class citizens were captured by the French Bulldog's specific brand of charm. However, members of high society soon began taking a fancy to them too, and over the following decades French Bulldogs were bought by the likes of the Russian royal family and high-powered American brokers. Meanwhile, the British did not take much interest – perhaps due to the French Bulldog's meagre working-class origins in England. Thus, the French were the proud custodians of the breed until the late 19th century when well-to-do Americans eagerly brought them to the United States and quickly featured them in the Westminster Dog Show, commencing in 1896. From their humble beginnings to the far reaches of society, nothing has since changed and the French Bulldog is still considered a breed for all people.

RUSSELL TOVEY
+ ROCKY

Russell Tovey speaks in a discreet, lowered timbre as he sits on the train from Edinburgh en route back home to London. He's gearing up for a demanding week of rehearsals for his stage performance in Constellations, amidst a handful of other creative projects including expanding on his passion for art through his bestselling book *Talk Art: Everything you wanted to know about contemporary art but were afraid to ask.* When describing how he finds the time for his array of eclectic endeavours, he quotes Noel Coward: 'When work is more fun than fun, you enjoy something and you're enthusiastic, you balance it. You compartmentalise and make the time.'

There's an earnest depth in Tovey's voice, insinuating wisdom beyond his years as he speaks with a softness about Rocky, his Blue French Bulldog and kindred old soul who has proved much more than a mere companion for the past nine years. Rocky has changed everything about the dynamic actor's life, as he expresses, 'He's the best thing that's ever happened to me. I tell him every day.' Rocky could have quite easily been a Rambo instead, as Tovey explains the quizzical Sylvester Stallone nod with an anecdote which could only be conjured up by a British thespian. 'I did a film called The Good Liar with Helen Mirren and Ian McKellen. Helen asked "Why Rocky?" I said, "Because it's kind of butch, but it's kind of camp at the same time." She replied, "Well, that's like you, darling." It's why I went with Rocky because it's a butch/camp combination."

Tovey's late-friend owned a Frenchie called Ernie, who he dog sat for. From then on, he fell completely in love with the breed's personality and felt an indescribable connection, 'This is what I need.' So,

Tovey diligently commenced his research – a non-negotiable when it comes to buying a new dog, particularly Frenchies. This is because the French Bulldog's increasing popularity in recent years has turned into a craze spurring many to make quick, uninformed purchases over Craigslist and through 'puppy brokers'. What it not often understood is the pervasiveness of unethical breeding in the industry propelled by the growing demand. From puppies without proper Kennel Club registration to lack of health testing by the breeder, there is a handful of key indicators denoting ill-breeding practices. Many female Frenchies are sadly treated like breeding-machines, ending up in rescue centres once they're unable to bear more litters.

This is why it's imperative to ensure the breeder is registered, request the parents' medical history and interview the breeder to ascertain their credibility. A respectable breeder should also ask the buyer questions to verify their puppies are going to good homes. It takes time and effort, but the benefit is bringing a healthy puppy into the home. For Tovey, these things were critical and he was able to source a reputable family breeder in North London. Upon his arrival, he found only two Frenchie puppies remained. He initially had his eye on Rocky's brother, adorned with a mohawk reminiscent of Stripe from the Gremlins movies. However, as they played, it soon became clear Stripe had a bite tendency, whilst Rocky ran around gleefully behind him. Tovey hoisted Rocky up, held him against his chest, and the doe-eyed pup sleepily closed his eyes and let out a fart. The deal was done. 'Well, there you go,' Tovey said. 'That's the one for me.'

Characteristically, Frenchies exude charm and wit, perhaps why a few years ago they sauntered up to the number one spot for breed desirability in England, overtaking tried-and-trusted Labradors. Rocky displays this affability and so much more. Tovey thoughtfully elaborates, 'He is very wise and very stubborn. He's selective with what he wants to listen to, he's food-obsessed, his cartoon-character eyes make it easy to manipulate your emotions to get what he wants. He is very clever. He's incredibly loyal with a really good sense of humour … he's everything!'

Dogs are emotionally sensitive animals with the cognitive ability to interpret the tone and inflections in our voice as well as our body movements, just as they would respond to the snaps and growls of an alpha wolf in the wild. Studies have been conducted showing dogs have the ability to assess human eye movement directing a command even better than chimpanzees or human infants. They are also evolutionarily wired to please their superior in order to maintain pack equilibrium. When combined, these traits comprise what we experience today as the finely domesticated canine. And Rocky, Tovey illustrates, is no exception to the rule. Rocky learns new tricks with ease and at nine years old has mastered the art of the Counting Game which Tovey and his partner invented during lockdown. Even more receptive than the most well-behaved child, Rocky has learnt to get to Tovey by the time he counts to five. Tovey remarks 'He now does it without even thinking about it. It's amazing. He's a very smart dog – it's as if he has been on this planet before.' Rocky's single vice is chasing footballs with abandon and he's known to halt local park matches, leaving Tovey bolting after him in his wake.

Rocky intrinsically improves the quality of Tovey's life and has helped him develop more mindful habits. Tovey illustrates, 'We had a family dog growing up so I knew what that was like. When I was a kid, I remember mum saying "Okay, you've got to take the dog for a walk" and I'd be like, "Eugh but I've just come back from school!" and now it's, "Okay, let's go for a little adventure … have a little sniff and a wee in the street." It's unexpected how much I look forward to going on a good walk with the dog.' Dogs ground us and bring us back to the present, and Rocky has elicited the very same within Tovey.

Balancing a strong workload and multiple pursuits isn't an easy feat in a city as busy as London in the 21st century. Dogs, like children, demand our time and resources, making us compromise in ways we could have never anticipated prior to taking on the responsibility. Tovey does everything in his ability to bring Rocky along with him everywhere he goes, including work functions. With the two Bassets and Tovey's partner at home, Rocky is never left alone for too long. He is also exceptionally well-behaved while joining Tovey at photoshoots and at times takes part in the action. Tovey conveys total transparency and great emotional maturity as he says/advises, 'You must be conscious of the time you have and the responsibility, but it's an absolute honour to be burdened with Rocky. Any compromise to adjust to know he's going to be okay isn't a compromise, it's just a necessity.'

There is the remaining question around the infamous health issues arising in French Bulldogs. There are a number of these potential concerns in Frenchies which many breeders are attempting to breed out. As Rocky ages, he has developed what Tovey denotes 'hop-skip-jump' as a result of spinal compression, affecting 95% of French Bulldogs. The breed also commonly develops a 'bunny hop', an early sign of hip dysplasia which although it looks cute, points to a potentially painful deterioration within the hip socket. Just like any elderly human, older dogs also suffer from aches and pains and Rocky's vet has advised Tovey to keep an eye on this. Many people looking to get a Frenchie may not be aware of these ailments and the integrity of the breeder is crucial, so research is key.

Tovey proffers advice for new dog owners from his own experiences owning a well-rounded Frenchie about town. He says the most important aspect of raising a dog is to train them to a point where they feel fully comfortable with you so they are happy to tag along in any situation. 'All my friends have seen my relationship with Rocky. I spent a lot of time training him and really enjoyed it. Now their expectation is to have that situation. I've been lucky as Rocky is a very special dog and I have also made sure we are bonded. I think one of the most challenging things is to make sure you bond with your dog to the point where they feel like you are their home wherever you are in the world, so you can take them anywhere.' From the photoshoots to the art galleries, Tovey has absolutely nailed it. Except if there are footballs involved.

THE
LABRADOR

The genesis of one of the world's most iconic and versatile breeds is surprisingly multi-layered. In the 1500s, resilient English settlers to Newfoundland brought hunting dogs along with them, who over time comingled to produce a breed the settlers named the St John's Water Dog. The most proficient among these dogs were bred for their talents for retrieving lines, rope and even nets filled to the brim with fish from the icy waters. Their coat had a particularly oily characteristic which acted as waterproofing in the freezing temperatures, while their webbed paws allowed them to swim with ease. What became the St John's Water Dog – with its black and white tuxedo-like coat – was the predecessor of all modern retrievers, including but not limited to the Flat-Coated Retriever, the Chesapeake Bay Retriever, the Golden Retriever and of course the Labrador Retriever. The Newfoundland is also said to derive from this lineage. The St John's Water Dog's enthusiasm for water-based retrieving was hailed by the fishermen and when the dogs accompanied them on shipping trips back to the United Kingdom, they would instruct them to perform their skills for curious onlookers. Soon, regular imports of these dogs were directed into Poole, on the south coast of England. This was where the Earl of Malmesbury witnessed the breed retrieving and was struck with an idea: the breed would be ideal for duck hunting on his estate. It was then his family established a breeding programme for the dog, which the Earl dubbed the Labrador. In 1903, the English Kennel Club recognised the breed and soon after their importation into the United States allowed American hunters and farmers to utilise the breed, eventually developing into a particular lineage of American Labrador Retrievers which have enhanced energy and a leaner physique. Today, Labradors are one of the most widley used working breeds in the world and are as eager in their roles as retrievers as they are when given the responsibility of acting as 'seeing eye' dogs and therapy dogs.

ALISTAIR PETRIE
+ MARA & ZOOEY

Exuding the style and artistic flow unique to thespians balanced with a grounded presence, actor Alistair Petrie transmutes his creative flair from screen to conversational storytelling. His tall frame houses a powerful yet understated quality as he selects a chair in his local country pub following a ramble around Frensham Little Pond, an enchantingly scenic spot he always enjoys exploring with Mara, his black Labrador, and Zooey, a Labrador-Alsatian cross. Petrie, most recently known for his role as the headmaster in the Netflix hit show Sex Education, has cultivated a 30-year career playing dynamic characters spanning theatre, television and film. Imbued with a heartfelt effusiveness, he reminisces about navigating the intricacies of dog ownership and the joys and trials therein. Petrie begins by recalling how his upbringing in a military family meant experiencing childhood in the constant throes of transience, rendering his deeply entrenched desire to own a dog unrealistic. The yearning proceeded into adulthood, although once married, he and his wife felt it was impractical and unfair to own a dog while living in London due to the lack of space. Thus, Petrie's patience for owning a pet continued to be exercised.

It was not until the Petrie family traded city life for the rolling countryside of Surrey that they felt the timing was right. Petrie's excitement peaked as he was clear on the perfect breed for his family: a Red Fox Labrador. Since spotting this particular breed in a Cornwall pub during a holiday, Petrie had been taken by the robust rust colour combined with the gentle demeanour and upbeat energy. This serendipitous happenstance was the leading inspiration for their first Labrador, Tilly. Labradors have proven to be one of the most enduringly popular breeds both in the United Kingdom and United States due to their versatility and intuitiveness, and they have unwaveringly claimed a 30-year number one spot as the most popular dog in the latter country. Therefore,

it is no surprise that the viscerally led Petrie was immediately struck by the qualities of this cherished breed. Tilly's gender was also carefully selected, as Petrie chortles, 'We had an abundance of testosterone with three boys in the household, so bringing a female in was a refreshing addition.'

Thoughtfully, Petrie acknowledges, 'Dogs teach you so much about yourself.' However, at times the lessons might not be the ones a person necessarily wishes for. Petrie admits to having smothered Tilly with affection due to his naturally tactile and tender nature. It was quickly apparent she found his perpetual nuzzling smothering and soon began gravitating towards his wife's desk. Over time, Tilly's reactions to his abundance of adoration taught Petrie, in his words: 'To allow dogs the space to simply be dogs.' Over-coddling, especially as puppies, can signal to the dog that co-dependence is the correct way which may cause clinginess and separation anxiety, over time proving difficult to rectify. People who show love for their dogs through excessive 'babying' often do not realise it can be detrimental to the development of their dog's sense of healthy separation. Ultimately, it is crucial a dog understands how to be away from its owner for regular amounts of time, and as Petrie says, 'to simply be a dog'.

Tilly taught Petrie not only this lesson in autonomy, but soon one much more heart wrenching. When Tilly reached adulthood, Petrie bred her with a black Labrador and she whelped nine healthy black puppies. Petrie fondly remarks, 'At the time of delivery, I was filming in Budapest for the television show The Terror. While on set, I received continuous updates on my phone when each puppy arrived.' The Petrie family adopted out each puppy except for the quietest and most sensitive one, who they named Mara after associated familial connections and love for the Maasai Mara.

Not long after the elation of receiving the puppies into their lives, tragedy struck. When the puppies were just four months old, Tilly was on heat and found a way to escape from their house. Though the Petrie home was nowhere near a main road, Tilly wandered far afield and was fatally struck by a car. Her death was momentous for the family, not only as Tilly was Petrie's first dog, but also as it was his boys' first experience with death. Petrie's 12-year-old son called him to relay the harrowing news as he sobbed into the phone. The boys were devastated and the decision was made to bury Tilly in the back garden by a tree where they placed a stone they had painted to reflect on the memory of their beloved pet. The family then consciously chose to focus their attention not on the tragedy, but on raising Tilly's legacy, Mara.

This difficult memory triggers Petrie to contemplate the notion of 'navigating one's life through dogs.' Although a philosophical sentiment, events like these are primary cornerstones for every dog owner. When the choice is made to bring a pet into the family, especially one embodying the affection and loyalty of a canine, oftentimes only the most sanguine moments are anticipated. It is not until an individual or family experiences the loss and associated grief for a dog that they can fully understand the weight and complexity of what it means to be a dog owner. When a child experiences his or her formative years with the companionship of a dog – to protect, to provide empathy and support, to be the welcoming face when arriving home from school – and the subsequent loss, it provides an entirely distinct layer to the child's emotional growth and maturity. Loss is one of the greatest teachers and the death of a treasured pet proves no exception.

A short time following Tilly's passing, Petrie felt it was important for Mara to grow up with a canine accomplice. When a friend realised the impracticality of owning her whippet in London, Petrie spontaneously offered to adopt her. Petrie formerly viewed whippets as elegant but lacking warmth, however his thoughts rapidly pivoted as he recalls Lenny was 'Heaven on a stick.' Mara was incredibly accepting of Lenny and they enjoyed each other's company; however tragedy struck again after 18 months of owning Lenny when she bolted during a walk and was hit by a car. This

proved yet another difficult lesson for the Petrie family and Mara was back on her own.

While Petrie was busy filming The Night Manager television series with Hugh Laurie, Laurie's wife heard of a new litter of Labrador-Alsatian crosses in Luton and chose one of the males. Petrie, never resisting a spontaneous opportunity especially when it comes to dogs, bought the sister pup who they named Zooey. Petrie describes Zooey as a particularly nuanced canine. He explains how the Alsatian comes through in that she shows an element of protectiveness and jealousy which Mara has never conveyed. If another dog comes up to Petrie for a pat, or if he and his wife have a hug, she shows her disproval. Zooey has no interest in chasing a stick, however enjoys chasing Mara chasing a stick. Petrie muses, 'Dogs are always present. It's like when you have a lovely relationship with someone and you know they're in the next room, it gives you reassurance. Every day, they reset – they don't wake up grumpy. Every day is the start of a great new day which sets you off.'

Describing how the family and dogs operate as a pack, Petrie delineates how each person has a role, and how the experience of dog ownership completely changed his children's formative years. 'When children grow up with dogs, they learn to have an intangible connection to something that isn't necessarily obvious because you can't ask a dog "Why are you doing that?" They simply demonstrate it.' Petrie's boys are encouraged to walk Zooey and Mara and conversations always end with '… and what about the dogs?' When they go on holiday, they always take them along as they are part of the pack.

Petrie advises that when a person chooses to be a dog owner, they must take on the dog's foibles as well as the responsibility. The owner needs to be aware when something is not quite right, being perceptive of the dog's moods and when their energy changes, which might indicate a health issue. Petrie strongly asserts, 'The individual has to be as present for their dogs as possible and factor them into every decision. If you can't, don't do it until you can.' When asked what the most unexpected thing is about being a dog owner, Petrie gushes, 'The relentless joy they give you. They're complicatedly uncomplicated but there's a joy in that. There's simplicity but it's a nuanced experience: emotionally and otherwise.'

THE
MIXED BREED

The mutt. The mongrel. The mixed breed. Until a few couple of decades ago, these terms typified a questionable connotation. It was deemed fashionable to own a canine with a fixed bloodline characterising a specific set of attributes – ones which the owner likely felt exemplified his or her own personality. However, in more recent years this trend has been turned on its head with the help of influential individuals acting as ambassadors and conscious campaigns. In an era where every aspect of western society encourages fluid identities and mutable personas, the mutt truly represents the multi-layered essence of today. So much so in fact, that many former mixed breeds funnelled into pedigree breeds of their own, such as the Labradoodle and Puggle. The benefits of owning a dog with a mixed bloodline are numerous. While pedigree dogs are prone to hereditary diseases as each descends from a small pool of predecessors – with inbreeding initially being required to retain the desired traits – mixed dogs have an advantage called hybrid vigour. This means a dog descended from separate gene pools does not exhibit the recessive genes which would otherwise present health issues. Thus, the all-too-common hip dysplasia often seen in Retrievers and German Shepherds and the plethora of heart diseases common in Dachshunds, Dobermans and Boxers would be far less of a concern for a new owner adopting a mixed canine of unknown heritage. Particular behavioural tendencies connected with a specific breed of dog can prove challenging, which further incentivises an owner to opt for a mutt as ill-favoured traits are toned down when various heritages interlap. It goes without saying that to adopt means to save a life. The rewards are ample – for both owner and the dog.

REMI WOLF
+ JUNO

From her irreverent anthems and the shock of hair to ceaselessly donning splashes of colour from head to toe, Remi Wolf never constrains herself to the ordinary. The same disregard for convention filters into her often spontaneous life choices, which she confesses are often galvanisers for growth. Wolf is currently in the midst of preparing for a global tour to promote her latest album, Juno. The gloriously wild array of pop-funk pieces is an ode to Generation Y overlaid with the upbeat, triumphant spirit greatly needed during the rollercoaster of the past two years. Wolf's Northern California casual manner intermingled with sincere unpretentiousness permeates through as she speaks on life, values and of course, the love of her life: her French Bulldog-Boston Terrier cross, Juno Jameson.

Wolf's array of dog-themed albums and EPs, including You're A Dog!, I'm Allergic to Dogs! And most recently Juno, arose from a single inside joke among friends long ago. Wolf's then-boyfriend was transitioning to veganism and during the process, lectured her on his view of how when a person eats a cow, it is akin to eating a dog. So, the ever-quirky Remi began rattling off to her friends, 'Cows are dogs', which became a running theme. The phrase finally diverged into simply 'You're a dog'. Wolf's dog fixation began long before the relationship, however. Her father, an enduring Labrador purist, ensured she grew up with the lovable breed so the family took on two black Labs, half-siblings Canon and Bida. Then, during university, Wolf co-fostered dogs and cats with ten other students while living in a share-house.

It was not until mid-March 2020 and the start of the pandemic, when Wolf felt it was the ideal time to take on a dog of her own. With a French Bulldog or Goldendoodle in mind, she browsed on the classified advertisement website Recycler and quickly discovered an ad for eight-week-old French Bulldog-Boston Terrier cross puppies. The very next day, she brought one of these puppies into her life and named him Juno Jameson – an ode to the iconic synthesiser and her favourite alcoholic beverage. A year and a half later, Juno has grown into a solid 18-kilogram (40-pound) dog with a Boston coat and pure Frenchie personality. Wolf remarks, 'Juno is cute, compact and just the perfect size. He is crazy and stubborn, which is typical of Frenchies.' Juno's stubbornness comes through especially when on a walk as, unless he is accompanied by another dog, he has no interest. Wolf laughs and comments on Juno's resemblance to a little pig as a large part of his personality is the abundance of loud noises he makes. Juno constantly snores as he naps and Wolf mentions he does have breathing difficulties at times – a trademark breeding shortcoming.

With such a dedication and affection for canines, it is hard to believe Wolf is allergic to dogs. She has simply accepted this throughout her life; however it worsened with Juno so she takes allergy medication to combat the symptoms. As she constantly finds herself around animals and having lived with Juno for over a year, she feels her symptoms have decreased over time, perhaps through her body adapting. 'There are times when I disregard medication and I believe my body has exposure therapy, so it does not impact me as it used to.' French Bulldogs, though currently one of the most popular urban dogs, are not the most fitting choice for people with allergies as the breed's commonplace skin issues coupled with moderate shedding easily exacerbate human allergies. Not actually caused by the fur itself, allergies to dogs are typically triggered by a protein within the dog's saliva and urine which melds to the dander on their skin. Therefore choosing a dog which does not moult as frequently – such as Wolf's original idea of a Goldendoodle – would be an ideal breed for those with allergies.

A number of breeds are known to suit those who are allergy-prone. Small breeds such as the Bichon Frise, Maltese Terrier, Miniature Poodle or Shih Tzu are well known for low shedding, while the same can be said for equally small but robust breeds like the Border Terrier and West Highland Terrier. It is important to keep in mind the fact a smaller dog naturally has a smaller amount of fur and dander than a large breed. For those with their eyes set on a larger dog, breeds such as Afghans, Portuguese Water Dogs, Standard Poodles and Soft Coated Wheaton Terriers do not moult, although they do require regular grooming. Ancient, unusual breeds such as the Basenji and Xoloitzcuintli are also low shedding – or in the latter case, no shedding – and could prove to be both a unique and beneficial option to inhibit allergy triggers.

Detailing the stark difference in breed popularity between Los Angeles and Northern California, Wolf explains, 'Dogs like Juno are quite trendy in Los Angeles as they do not require wide open spaces to exist happily so are therefore perfect for city apartments.' Wolf grew up in suburban, family-oriented Palo Alto which maintains a more traditional outlook on breed selection. 'Labradors, Golden Retrievers, Poodles and Cocker Spaniels are the standard Palo Alto-type dog. Smaller dogs like Yorkies and Chihuahuas have much more popularity in Los Angeles. Even Pit Bulls have become a family dog in Southern California.' Wolf expresses how the dog culture in Los Angeles emphasises rescuing from shelters. 'It is common here in LA for people to put so much work into their dogs' rehabilitation from past traumas and at times from previous owners. I haven't seen this culture anywhere else. In the Bay Area, it is not the norm to go to a shelter as people simply gravitate towards breeders.' Wolf suggests it could be due to less shelters being available in Northern California and difficult adoption which could bar people from opting for the rescue route.

Like Los Angeles, Great Britain is world-renowned for its fervent dog culture. It is estimated seven out of ten people in England would consider adoption over buying from a breeder and with the process digitally streamlined over the years, it has become even more convenient for people to locate dogs in need. However, this ease of adoption can prove a double-edged sword if not carefully considered. During the pandemic, dog adoptions soared as individuals sought to temper their loneliness and isolation with a new pet, and for many, it was the exact cure they needed. Meanwhile, many pets were filling shelters at a similar rate because the convenience of easy adoption also meant at times spur-of-the-moment choices were made and then regretted later. This is sadly due to not having an understanding or preparedness for behavioural or health issues. To bring a dog into a home and only later realise hidden traits and health concerns is always a possibility, so empathy should be underpinning the entire dog ownership experience.

For Wolf, the support of her family means Juno is always considered as his ownership is in part shared when necessary. When planning a tour, the initial hope to bring him along was changed to her parents looking after him. 'I feel he would be happier spending time with my mom and dad, and of course their new Chocolate Labrador puppy, Lucky. Juno is very protective of him.' Wolf addresses how this will be the ideal situation as Juno adores the dog park and will frolic around for hours without tiring, an experience her parents will gladly provide for him. Wolf's mother is also an avid dog lover and fostered dogs throughout the pandemic so Juno will never be short of attention.

Through her music, Wolf strives to break boundaries. Challenging the status quo, her personality is naturally brimming with an integral exuberance and precociousness. However, she reveals the cultivation of certain traits in recent times thanks to Juno. 'I feel I have become a more tolerant and loving person. Juno has made me much more open.' Wolf divulges how the love she feels for Juno also transmits into other areas of her life: 'As soon as I took Juno in, I began experiencing love on a deeper level because never before did I have to take care of anything on that level.' She explains how she felt she developed much more gratitude for everything around her. 'Dogs are incredibly pure and innocent – they're just a bright light shining into your life.'

THE
TOY POODLE

Despite the age-old stereotype of the Toy Poodle as a delicate, demanding breed, it is as dedicated as a Collie and as trainable as a German Shepherd. It is perhaps due to the surprising waterfowl hunting roots of its Standard Poodle ancestors that it has developed such a keen athleticism and prowess in the show ring. For this reason, the Poodle – originally christened Pudel by the Germans who bred them into their current form – is revered as one of the brightest and mentally developed canines out of approximately 365 breeds recognised by the USA's United Kennel Club today. As they hardly shed and therefore produce less dander, the breed is sought after by individuals with sensitive allergies, although their high-maintenance grooming requirements can make would-be owners think twice. It is expected that a Poodle companion will need to frequent the groomer's clipping studio every four to six weeks, with regular brushing in between to remove any excess fur. The grooming styles are simply endless. The simplest cut is called the Sporting Clip which moulds naturally around the dog's body, while the ostentatious Continental Clip is favoured by owners seeking to parade their dog around the showring. Other amusing variations include the English Saddle and Scandinavian Clip. One of the most intriguing aspects of the Toy Poodle is its sense of humour which trickles into its distinctly mischievous character. This same propensity for mischief makes mental stimulation mandatory and therefore agility training is a suitable undertaking for the energetic, performance-minded Toy Poodle who loves nothing more than the applause of a crowd.

KATY & SAEED AL-RUBEYI
+ PARTY

For Katy and Saeed Al-Rubeyi, choices made with ethical intention are the seeds of creating an ever more mindful world. Their brand Story MFG brings together a longstanding affinity for vintage throwbacks interwoven with a passion for sustainable textiles. Their approach to business development is equally as organic as their eco-conscious wares. Story MFG's grassroots beginnings saw them cultivating a humble crowdsourcing effort, which produced a small batch of jeans utilising natural dyes and fabrics. Eight years on, Story MFG is well recognised for blending social activism with the world of fashion through careful selection of vegan materials, agricultural conscientiousness and a rigorous zero-waste manufacturing process. The couple also lead by example through maintaining a staunch aim to uphold a cruelty-free lifestyle, which factored into their decision to rescue a Toy Poodle who has altered their lives in the most unanticipated of ways.

Party was given her name by the Al-Rubeyis to provide her with a clean slate and new lease of life after a traumatic past. Saeed had his mind set on a Poodle as he grew up with the breed and found them to be exceptionally clever in addition to hypoallergenic, nullifying the added need for shedding maintenance. For him, a Poodle was the practical choice. However, when the couple discovered this young three-kilo black-and-white bundle on a rehoming website during London's pandemic lockdown, they could have never anticipated the aggregation of complex behaviour issues. Saeed explicates, 'The first night we thought, "What have we done?" Owning a dog radically changes a person's life. It is why taking the time to assess whether it's the right fit in someone's life is key. Katy and I both owned dogs before, but Party was a completely different story.'

Rescue dogs are akin to humans in that they each exhibit distinct personalities. This is why it is crucial for the potential owner to pose questions about the dog's history so they can attempt to understand what they are working with and whether they can shoulder the responsibility. A dog tends to directly reflect its owner, thus when a person adopts, the complex blueprint of the previous owner is taken on as well. When Katy and Saeed rescued Party, the previous owners claimed she was properly house trained with no accompanying behavioural issues. It was not until the couple brought her home that they realised this information was entirely misleading. Party was not properly trained and suffered from severe separation anxiety which the Al-Rubeyis contended with for months on end. While they were not fully aware of her prior circumstances, they believe the owners did not care for her nutrition as her teeth were in poor condition. Saeed admits, 'Party's health in particular has been incredibly high maintenance and costly … we adopted her because she was adorable but then realised that we did not know how to handle her. She didn't have a great start and we have had to deal with the consequences.'

While choosing a dog without knowing their background can prove a liability, pedigree dogs do not escape their share of shortcomings. Buying pedigree ensures predictability around size, temperament and grooming needs, allowing the owner to feel confident not only that the dog will fit into their lifestyle but also that they have the capability to handle the needs of the breed. However, the method by which this predictability is achieved has an underlying disadvantage. Many purebreds pass on specific health and behavioural weaknesses due to the lack of genetic diversity inherent in selective breeding. To ensure certain traits are passed on in the bloodline, some breeders practice inbreeding for multiple generations, resulting in genetic defects which may not be readily apparent. In addition to the premium price tag for purebreds, these potential factors are not to be taken lightly.

With the popularity of celebrities opting to rescue rather than buy, the public has begun to view mixed breeds as equally desirable to purebreds. This is a step towards ethical awareness as mixed breeds are not only more genetically diverse, mitigating breed-specific health issues, but as rescue shelters overflow with unwanted dogs the need to consider adoption becomes ever more vital. While rescue dogs may demonstrate with their own set of problems, it is up to dog owners to work with these issues if they have the means and capability to do so. There is a beauty in overcoming the challenge of working with a dog while instilling the trust which it may not have previously had. The Al-Rubeyis experienced great success through working closely with Party's behavioural idiosyncrasies. 'We invested in a trainer who recommended when Party acts up to not engage or laugh at what she is doing since she goes into "entertainment mode", but we failed at this completely as she is hilarious with an enormous personality. This is juxtaposed to the early days when we thought she was simply a fearful dog.'

Saeed laughs as he describes Party's fully unleashed personality as 'cunningly manipulative'. Katy says, 'She is so clever; she is truly the lady boss of the house. She is completely affectionate and only cares about food and cuddles. She has to be touching one of us at all times and whenever we are eating, she always finds resourceful ways to get food. This is a complete contrast to how she was in the beginning.' Saeed reveals Party despises baths which is why they keep her on a low-maintenance cut requiring a full groom with a trim every six weeks, explaining, 'If she had a typical Poodle cut, she would have to be brushed each night, washed every ten days, then groomed every three weeks. She would loathe the experience.'

At just over two years old, the multifaceted Party has recently experienced yet another lifestyle adjustment: the arrival of the Al-Rubeyis' now five-month-old baby boy. Only three days after adopting Party, Katy fell pregnant and the couple describes the circumstances as 'incredibly hard work taking care of a high-maintenance traumatised dog alongside our first baby.' They reflect on feeling anxious about becoming first-time parents, but Party assisted them with this as she provided such a demanding experience which taught them valuable parenting lessons. When asked about Party's reaction to their new addition, Katy quips, 'Party completely ignores him and could not care less. She can't eat him and he can't give her cuddles. It is just fortunate she is not threatened by him. She likes his stinky diapers and that is the extent of her interest!' Though Party has never once displayed aggressive tendencies, they take the necessary precautions and never leave the two together without supervision.

Katy comments, 'It will be interesting to see how Party reacts once the baby grows and becomes tactile with her. We simply want him to grow up loving animals.' Alongside assisting the development of empathy and responsibility in children, growing up with dogs can aid a child's physical health. Studies have shown dogs strengthen children's immune systems from three months old, notably protecting against asthma and allergies. While all animals have this beneficial effect, dogs in particular add 56 various types of good bacteria and microbiomes to the home while cats add only 24 types. With the increase in childhood allergies in recent decades, this confirms how inherently beneficial it is for children to grow up with canine companions.

As vegans, the Al-Rubeyis assumed they would feed Party accordingly. Prior to her adoption, they spoke with dog owners throughout the UK, India and Thailand who promote vegan dog food which informed Party's initial food regime. However, they soon realised that as she suffers from major intestinal issues, consuming regular dog food was best for her. After undertaking additional research, they found raw meat would be most beneficial for her condition. For over eight years, meat had not been brought into the Al-Rubeyi household so this was initially a shock. Saeed discusses, 'The way we see it, veganism is our choice as well as a privilege. There are plenty of people who cannot access, afford or for health reasons consume vegan food, and Party is just one of these individuals. Her health comes first. We simply want her to have a good quality of life.'

It is a sincere act of responsibility for a dog owner to accept the needs of their dog while compromising on their personal beliefs. The conscientious couple chose to be unselfish in their quest to provide Party with the best life possible and though it appears to contradict their vegan values, it actually lends to those same values as their ethics transcend dogma. As for canines without health complications, a vegan diet could be a healthy alternative. Similar to humans, a plant-based approach minimises digestive problems, hypothyroidism and cancer risk. A dog's elimination pungency also decreases, which is a considerable benefit for any dog owner. On the other hand, a dog's digestive tract is not built for a plant-based diet and for a canine to receive essential nutrients, meals must be fortified with additional vitamins. It is therefore crucial to speak with a veterinarian prior to making the decision to switch a dog to a vegan regime.

After the immense amount of time and effort the Al-Rubeyis invested into Party, they now say she is a wonderful and rewarding addition to their home. Saeed laughs, 'For the first year, Party despised me and now she loves me even more than Katy. If I pat her and suddenly stop, she uses her paw to pull my hand back to her tummy.' He continues, 'It's similar to having a child. It is ultimately rewarding but an incredible amount of responsibility.' When asked whether Story MFG are planning to bring out a dog-wear line, Saeed alludes to it being in the works. They have even recently incorporated Party into the Story MFG narrative as she will be hand-embroidered on a sweater and t-shirt which will be released soon. From sombre beginnings to featuring on a fashion line, Party's story proves there is hope for every rescue dog as long as the owner's belief and dedication persevere.

THE PUG

Much contention surrounds the origins of the Pug. However, there remains one clear fact: for the past 2,500 years their purpose has solely been as a companion for the highest respected members of society. The most credible narrative is impressive to say the least. The Pug was deliberately bred to exhibit the most pleasing traits as a lap dog for Chinese monarchs during the dynasties existing between 782 and 150 BCE. Emperors were particularly fond of the noble yet humorous breed as they provided both affection and entertainment for their masters. The Chinese royals believed placing a sculpture of a stylised Pug, known to them as the Fu Dog, at the entrance of a sacred space such as a tomb or temple would ward off any visitor with less than benevolent intent. Another existing theory surmises that at around the same time Tibetan monks kept Pugs in a similar fashion – as comrades as well as guards in their monasteries. It is said Pugs were so highly prized, they had permanent wardens who would see to their protection. The breed's recognisably wrinkled features retain their own dignified purpose. Forehead lines in the shape of the Chinese symbol for 'prince' were bred into the dogs over time for additional veneration. In the 16th century, the Pug's acclaim swept across nations as the exceptional breed was taken to the Netherlands by the Dutch East India Trading Company and were soon seen by the side of European royals, leading to the Pug's popularity with the upper echelons of society during the Victorian era. From China and Tibet to Holland and England, the Pug has transcended the ages and has always done so in style.

ANDREW & MATTHEW
+ MR GREENBERG

Andrew Goetz and Matthew Malin, founders of leading skincare brand Malin+Goetz, understand how to masterfully manage complexity. Since the company's New York inception in 2004, they have combined the highest quality, naturally sourced ingredients with advanced technology to address dermal concerns worldwide. By doing away with cumbersome skincare regimes, Malin and Goetz provide an uncomplicated antidote to the finicky needs of sensitive skin. The couple's values as committed dog owners integrally align with their business mindset as they elicit a charming perspective on life with Mr Greenberg, their rescue Pug who has come with his own personal set of sensitivities.

The now eight-year-old Mr Greenberg was adopted from Vermont's Green Mountain Pug Rescue. Goetz explicates the delightfully circuitous etymology: 'Vermont is the French word for Green Mountain. The German word for mountain is berg, and since he is of course a New Yorker, there's the Jewish throwback. So: Greenberg.' Their choice of a Pug stemmed from their particular affinity and history with flat-nosed canines. Prior to Mr Greenberg, they owned an English and a French Bulldog, respectively named Bob and Junior. Having experienced those breeds, the single aspect the couple were not as fond of was the difficulty presented while travelling with an English Bulldog, due to his size. Goetz reminisces, 'After Bob passed away, Junior was with us for another year and we thoroughly enjoyed the ease of travelling with such a petite dog.' As Malin and Goetz's work requires a jet-setting itinerary, the decision to adopt

a similar sized breed provided them with the benefit of transportability, making their lives much easier. Sharing some background information acquired from his many years spent living in Holland, Goetz explains 'The folklore is that when the Spanish were invading Holland, the King of Holland owned a Pug who could sense the intruders and barked to awaken the king. It was because of this "noble" Pug that Holland was saved.'

Rescuing a canine is a noble decision, especially for those who have only had previous experience owning dogs bought from breeders. Malin and Goetz both felt it was the most compassionate choice after owning purebreds Bob and Junior. After investing time researching rescue centres, they discovered Green Mountain Pug Rescue, located only two hours away from their Hudson Valley residence. The couple describe the seamless experience of adopting Mr Greenberg. They phoned Green Mountain Pug Rescue to ascertain the best time for them to travel to the centre to view the available Pugs. The representative asked various questions about their home and work situation, then upon determining which Pug would best for them, enthusiastically offered, 'You don't even need to come to us, we will bring him to you to see how he works in your home!' Malin and Goetz say it was not their specific intent to adopt a Pug, it simply came down to happenstance and Mr Greenberg being a lapdog with the perfect temperament. They admit, 'We did not know anything about the breed before we adopted Mr Greenberg, but were of course aware of the spectrum of issues flat-nosed dogs contend with.'

Pugs are known to be full of charm and character, with the portability-factor which Malin and Goetz suggest. In terms of personality and logistics, this makes them an absolutely ideal companion for many modern families. However, while their flat-nose proves a charming feature, it is also the cause of a number of health concerns. Brachycephalic Obstructive Airway Syndrome, occurring in breeds with significantly short skull architecture, can result in the obstruction of the airways, meaning their ability to breathe becomes more difficult over time. Signs that a Pug is not able to breathe properly include excessive mouth breathing, snoring and increased panting. As the Pug breed tends to boast a voracious appetite, excess weight can exacerbate any breathing difficulties. As the couple have experienced other flat-nosed canines prior to Mr Greenberg, they understand the importance of keeping check on any developing issues while also maintaining the crucial regime of cleaning his ears and skin folds each week to ensure they do not become infected. Fortunately, Malin and Goetz describe Mr Greenberg as being in peak health without any allergies or ailments to date.

Malin softly offers, 'Mr Greenberg is the most kind-hearted, funny, neurotic and needy dog so we truly put all of our attention on him. It is a mutually beneficial relationship.' Mr Greenberg's favourite pastime is frisbee which he enjoys in the park, and as he is from Vermont, he is particularly accustomed to cold climates. When the temperature drops below tolerable, he dons his Burberry sweater – a hand-me-down from Junior. In terms of the trials of adopting, Goetz asserts, 'It is difficult to understand prior circumstances. Mr Greenberg was wonderful, however he did come with separation anxiety. It took a long time for him to be okay with us simply leaving for dinner.'

The most critical aspect of adopting, Malin and Goetz assert, is to choose a breed – or breed mix – which matches the person's lifestyle. 'There is so much work within the adjustment and transition period. It took us a full year before Mr Greenberg was comfortable where we could leave him without him going crazy. People do not often understand the commitment of helping an animal adjust into your life. They are soulful beings needing a tremendous amount of love.' Mr Greenberg is fortunate to experience close to constant engagement with his owners, however if an individual is away from their dog too often it will prove detrimental for the dog. Whilst researching rescues, the couple witnessed the profuse number of Pit Bulls in need of homes. They explain if their lifestyle had been different, they might have chosen one but when travelling between retail stores in cities across the world, it would just not be possible. Even Mr Greenberg had his share of troubles at the onset. Malin explains, 'Initially we brought Mr Greenberg into our main store in New York but because of his separation anxiety, he would bark at customers not as they came in but as they were leaving.' The quirks which rescue dogs might come with are opportunities for the owner to bond through training and developing trust, just as Malin and Goetz have done.

With Malin+Goetz stores popping up around the world – London, New York, Los Angeles, San Francisco and Hong Kong – it means the couple are always hopping around various offices. They manage to incorporate Mr Greenberg into the shorter six-hour trips to London and Los Angeles without any issue. He even enjoys partaking in many of their photoshoots. The duo also encourages their employees to bring their dogs into the office as they understand the importance of a dog's time spent with its owner. Amidst the couple's busy schedule, Mr Greenberg never fails to keep step as he is a keen traveller, whether in a basket or by bicycle, subway, Amtrak train or plane. Malin chortles, 'The only thing he is not great at is riding in the car. Every weekend we take a car trip and he goes absolutely berserk. He cannot contain himself so we have to put him in his carry case where he barks for the entire two-hour journey. So, in the car he becomes Mr Screamberg.'

The couple's favourite memory of Mr Greenberg is instantly recollected. An Italian business partner once gifted them a panettone for Christmas which was left within reach of Mr Greenberg. When the couple left the room, Mr Greenberg consumed the entire package, resulting in his defecating of panettone for weeks afterwards. Mr Greenberg's penchant for stealing food is not limited to the household. He enjoys stealing low-hanging fruit from the garden and is a keen diner of raspberries, blackberries and his favourite delicacy, tomatoes. It is lucky for Mr Greenberg that his stomach can sustain his obsession with fruit as many dogs' digestive systems cannot tolerate fruit dried in the sun.

In terms of Mr Greenberg's grooming routine, his requirements demand only a once per month at-home ritual, in his own dedicated bathtub of course. It goes without saying Mr Greenberg is bathed in Malin+Goetz dog shampoo, inspired by Bob and Junior. As the overriding principle for all Malin+Goetz products is making skincare easy and uncomplicated for the most sensitive of skin, the main focus of the dog shampoo is hydration and moisturising without skin irritation. The dog shampoo is close to human-grade quality and simply tweaked for canines. Using dog-specific shampoos should not be understated as anything else can easily create an imbalance in dogs' naturally high pH levels, leading to skin irritation. Malin and Goetz prescribe to the scientifically-backed idea that dogs should not be over-washed. Malin explains, 'Dogs lick themselves as it is a way for them to ingest vitamin D from oils secreted from glands in their skin. If you wash it away too often, they will not ingest the necessary vitamin D crucial for their health.'

This level of knowledge and care that Malin and Goetz integrate into their products is reflected in their commitment to Mr Greenberg. It is one thing to buy or adopt a dog. It is another thing to invest one's time and energy into compromising needs, adjusting expectations and adapting a lifestyle to fulfil the promise made the moment a person chooses to bring a canine companion into their life. While rescuing a dog can come with its own risks, outcomes such as Malin and Goetz have experienced with Mr Greenberg are testament to the tremendous reward.

THE
SHIBA INU

Japan's geological isolation created the perfect conditions the emergence of six unique Spitzes of a range of sizes, bred to be fervent hunters. Since the prehistoric Jōmon period of 14,000–900 BC, Japanese dogs have assisted the Jōmon people when hunting, an inherited drive which has been passed on to all Japanese dog breeds today. In around 500 AD Japanese dogs began to be utilised for ridding grain stores of rats in addition to their hunting roles, which further integrated the dogs into everyday life in Japan. However, after centuries of using Japanese dogs for hunting, in the mid-1800s the sudden influx of foreigners meant European breeds began to dominate the hunting scene in Japan, with native breeds almost forgotten. Fortunately, in 1928 Dr Hiroyoshi Saito recognised the importance of protecting Japanese dog breeds and for the first time in history began detailing and naming them. The detailed breeds, from largest to smallest, comprised the Akita, Kishu, Hokkaido, Shikoku, Kai and of course, the Shiba Inu. Three slightly divergent Shiba Inus which naturally existed in different locations across Japan were documented, each with varying physical features but all with very much the same temperament. Dr Saito's umbrella term for these dogs was Shiba, meaning 'brushwood', which points to their role in assisting Japanese hunters in the Chūbu mountains, capturing small game amongst the brush. Fast forward to the onset of World War II and the Shiba Inu population almost faced decimation due to mass bombing raids. The Shibas which survived the war contended with viral distemper which ran rampant throughout Japan in the post-war years. The ensuing strategy to rekindle the Shiba Inu population was to take the remaining bloodlines from the Japanese countryside to establish breeding programmes which resulted in a successful mission. The Shiba Inus of today all hark back to these origins and their dynamic, multi-layered past nods to a sense of entrenched nostalgia for Japanese owners of these richly historic dogs.

JAPAN

To this day, the diminutive and clever Shiba Inu has overarchingly remained the most popular breed in Japan. With its trademark orange coat (alongside the black-and-white coat variations), coiled tail and delightfully narrowed eyes, one's mind turns directly to a fox. Even the plush fur, with its robust double layering, is uncannily fox-like in appearance. And, like a fox, Shiba Inus are inherently cunning and crafty, lending to their particular uniqueness as a family pet. As they require ample mental stimulation and energy release, when left unattended for extended periods of time without adequate attention and exercise they can easily become destructive – without showing an inkling of apology or self-reproach once their owner returns. When taken outdoors to exert themselves, Shiba Inus will channel their instinctive ability to move with both poise and swiftness. Once back in the homestead, the Shiba Inu will deftly switch to embodying a much more tranquil and softer temperament – albeit still with the cunning eye of a fox.

The Shiba Inu's breed standard details them as displaying spirited boldness, good nature and artlessness – qualities which although intriguing, may not prove the most ideal for all household situations. Yet another comparison commonly made is the Shiba Inu's similarity to a feline in that they prefer to remain aloof and can often be found cleaning themselves as they have an inherent aversion to dirtiness. This hygienic preoccupation also means they are easy to housetrain and even as puppies, they prefer to not soil inside anywhere close to where they sleep. This feature is coincidentally consistent with Japan's hygienic, meticulously organised culture. However, an intriguing aspect of the Shiba Inu's popularity, in addition to its history, is the love of Shibas as a counter to the culture, a concept represented by animé and manga. Japan's predilection for animé stems in part from the fact that Japanese expectations are set at such a high bar – with respect for all things coordinated, structured and efficient – that the innocent reprieve from this standard is to embrace that which is deemed cute, colourful and uninhibited. The Shiba Inu itself epitomises these exact attributes. So in a sense, the Shiba Inu represents its culture as much as it represents a contradistinction to the culture.

Though becoming particularly trendy throughout the world as their foxy appearance is a sought-after quality, the Shiba Inu's uniqueness and particular idiosyncrasies cannot be overlooked. As they are such a petite size, topping out at only 9 kg (20 lb) in weight and reaching only 40 cm (15 inches) in height, they are well suited to apartment living. However, due to centuries of embedded hunting drive, the need for exercise cannot be stressed enough. This means an owner who has a keenness for running would be an ideal companion for the Shiba Inu breed. And in line with their inherited hunting instinct, they typically do not fare well with smaller pets in the household as they have an innate desire to chase. This prey drive is difficult to train out and as the Shiba Inu is an incredibly intelligent breed, training in a general sense can prove difficult. As Shibas are naturally autonomous dogs who value their freedom, using training methods which play on these traits is typically quite successful. Establishing rules as a base approach is integral to their training as they are instinctually dominant and will test their owner's leadership ability. Further, the breed is known for its aggression towards other canines and as they can be possessive of their owners, proper socialisation from puppyhood is an absolute necessity. The most curious aspect of the Shiba Inu is undoubtedly the 'Shiba scream' it emits when displeased or excited, which can be startling when its owner is caught off guard.

Those who own Shiba Inus are proud to be associated with such a special breed. Their fiery and bold personalities radiate amongst more traditional dog breeds and their owners are often entertained by their complex natures. They are arguably one of the most independently minded canines and tend to relish challenging their owners when they do not agree with a request made of them. This means only owners who have the necessary alpha ability should consider taking on a Shiba Inu lest the canine rules the household. Would-be owners of these one-of-a-kind dogs should be in the market for a canine which will keep them on their toes – they are definitely not for the faint of heart or first-time dog owners. Plenty of mental stimulation and puppy training classes are critical to raising a well-rounded and socialised Shiba Inu, so if time or resources are limited, it is advised against bringing this high-maintenance breed into the household. The Shiba's loyalty to their family, however, is second to none and though they will endlessly test boundaries, they remain steadfastly devoted to their owner. It's everyone else they prefer not to consider.

THE
WHIPPET

Is there any dog more emblazoned into the history books and art galleries as profusely as the venerable Whippet? From its beginnings in the fields of England, eagerly hunting hares for their noble masters, the elegant canine's primary usage has always been harnessing its speed and agility across terrain. As one of the leading members of the Sighthound canine classification, including but not limited to Greyhounds, Borzoi and Salukis, they are primarily guided by their keen sense of sight rather than by smell. It goes without saying their aesthetic appeal merged nicely with the aristocracy, their lithe curvature and natural grace exuding a sense of refinement. Curiously, however, the Whippet was once thought of as the 'poor man's Greyhound', due to the fact that northern English working class who were not able to afford proper Greyhounds were instead offered this petite version, allegedly bred with small Terriers. This intermixing proved a benefit rather than hindrance as the owners would take their dogs to the countryside on their days off and, using the bribe of a waving piece of cloth, raced them in what became known as 'rag racing'. It is said that the Greyhound's mix with the Terrier led the Whippet to achieve the scrappiness required to win these races. Over time, Whippet rag racing attracted wider attention across England and overseas, which developed into international events. The Whippet's growing popularity meant that by 1891 The Kennel Club of the UK finally officially recognised the breed, bestowing upon them entry into esteemed dog shows. Times have now changed and this exceptionally amiable and docile breed can most often be seen relaxing placidly across their owners' laps or curled up on any warm, fluffy surface in the home. Though they appreciate a solid sprint in nature, they love nothing more than to retreat back to the comfort of their family. Whippets have been and always will be the archetypal devoted member of the dog world.

ROSIE BIRKETT
+ CYRIL

New Year's Eve was the night Rosie Birkett serendipitously met the man who would become her husband. It was in the same evening he expressed his plans to embark on a two-year working holiday experience in Canada, set to leave in just a couple of months' time. A whirlwind romance quickly developed, prompting the spontaneous idea for the food writer and broadcaster to join him – a decision ultimately made sweeter by Vancouver's vibrant and growing food scene. While experiencing life in Canada, they shared a home with a Frenchman named Cyril – who instead being of a hindrance to their new romance proved to be a muse of sorts. Rosie softly reminisces, 'Cyril was absolutely lovely and taught me how to make galettes. He was so considerate and great to be around; we really loved him.' When the couple returned to the UK the following year, Cyril came back into the picture – but only in spirit. Rosie had always dreamt of having a dog, while her husband remained hesitant due to the commitment and responsibility owning a dog demands. After time, she managed to talk him around and not long after they began to explore the perfect dog name. The name Cyril, they decided, would be simply perfect, perhaps cultivating the energy of a dog with the gentle, courteous and loving personality of their former French housemate.

Rosie conveys how researching to discover the right breeder was of highest importance. 'I was conscious of not buying a puppy from someone who didn't value the welfare of the mother...a breeder only doing it for the money.' This is all too common an occurrence as dog breeding has infamously become a profit-driven exercise and is the primary reason why proper research is paramount when setting out on the path to choose a breeder. So, in August of 2014, Rosie diligently investigated online and came upon a Whippet breeder in Leicester. The breeder had just bred two dogs for the first time and knew both the mother and father well – an important aspect of breeder selection, as they should be able to illustrate commitment and investment in both the puppies and their parents. From the beginning, Rosie had her mind set on a owning a solid blue male, however by the time she made contact with the breeder only the parti-coloured blue-and-white male remained. The moment the breeder sent a photo of him to Rosie, her previous expectation completely melted away and she simply could not resist the puppy – and just as importantly, nor could her husband. They drove to Leicester and on arrival, they discerned how integrous the breeder was through viewing her premises and asking the right questions. And they named the little parti-coloured pup Cyril.

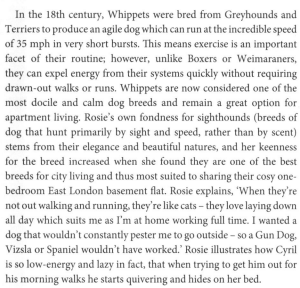

In the 18th century, Whippets were bred from Greyhounds and Terriers to produce an agile dog which can run at the incredible speed of 35 mph in very short bursts. This means exercise is an important facet of their routine; however, unlike Boxers or Weimaraners, they can expel energy from their systems quickly without requiring drawn-out walks or runs. Whippets are now considered one of the most docile and calm dog breeds and remain a great option for apartment living. Rosie's own fondness for sighthounds (breeds of dog that hunt primarily by sight and speed, rather than by scent) stems from their elegance and beautiful natures, and her keenness for the breed increased when she found they are one of the best breeds for city living and thus most suited to sharing their cosy one-bedroom East London basement flat. Rosie explains, 'When they're not out walking and running, they're like cats – they love laying down all day which suits me as I'm at home working full time. I wanted a dog that wouldn't constantly pester me to go outside – so a Gun Dog, Vizsla or Spaniel wouldn't have worked.' Rosie illustrates how Cyril is so low-energy and lazy in fact, that when trying to get him out for his morning walks he starts quivering and hides on her bed.

Whippets' affectionate natures are renowned. They are typified as one of the most sensitive breeds, with Rosie describing them as 'incredibly gentle and tactile'. She elaborates, 'They're different from any other kind of dog with a very unique nature and way of being. Cyril is like more of a creature than a dog. His nickname is Mr Shmoo because he's more of a shmoo than a dog.' Cyril can be quite playful, barking along while his owners sing the old football song to him, Nice One, Cyril. He will also lay down beside Rosie to console her when he senses she is upset. His sensitive nature can at times translate into neediness and anxiety, as he always follows Rosie and her husband around the house. During car trips, he developed a behaviour similar to a panic attack – including distressed panting and profuse salivating – which has halted them from being able to take him along during car trips. In puppyhood, Cyril went through a stage of severe separation anxiety, but Rosie went to the lengths of recording her voice on a loop which soothes him when they would go out. Rosie reveals, 'It was a test on our relationship because it was so much responsibility so early on when we first got together.' Many dog breeds are prone to bouts of anxiety, however this is breed-specific for Whippets. Using methods such as a Kong Ball filled with peanut butter, leaving some recently-worn clothes in the dog bed or using natural dog-friendly calming remedies can all prove helpful. However, when the case is more serious, a dog behaviouralist's intervention may be required. An important aspect of dog ownership is realising, as Rosie explains, how each dog is so individual and needs to be tended to according to their particular needs.

Due to her work in the food industry, Rosie is undoubtedly invested in providing Cyril with proper nutrition to maintain his peak health. When asked how she chooses the right dog food, she reveals her desire to keep him away from processed foods, 'As a hunting dog he needs substantial protein. So we started him on poached chicken but soon realised he has allergies to chicken, salmon and wheat.' This ushered in a change in direction with Cyril's diet, and Rosie exchanged chicken for a ground beef and dry kibble combo. They felt Cyril should have something completely natural, nutritious and mindful of his allergies, so they now feed him Forthglade, an all-natural dog food brand based in Devon which omits fillers and preservatives.

Cyril's appetite is not always all-naturally oriented, however. Rosie divulges, 'Cyril is a bit naughty with food…He's obsessed with eating anything he's not meant to, the stinkier and more grotesque the better. He's a scavenger and whenever we are on a walk, he scavenges for fish bones and anything he can find. Unspeakable things.' Through evolution, dogs and cats have both developed the same number of receptors in their brain which detect the taste of bitterness, preventing them from ingesting environmental toxins. Meanwhile, cats' brains are unable to detect sweetness in food and although they have the same number of bitterness receptors as dogs, these receptors are even more sensitive to bitter flavours than other mammals. This is the reason cats tend to be more discerning of what they eat compared with dogs. Moreover, when a dog eats another animal's waste, it can be an indicator of nutritional deficiency due to malabsorption or an unbalanced diet, though they could simply enjoy the taste as dogs are neophilic, meaning they enjoy whatever is new and interesting to them.

In the midst of cooking brownies and writing a cookbook in their East London flat, she happened to look away only for a minute to find Cyril had run over to eat them. She was horrified and rushed him to the vet as chocolate is notably dangerous for dogs. Unfortunately this is something she has had to do many times due to Cyril's love of sneakily consuming forbidden treats. On another occasion, Cyril surreptitiously broke into a Fortnum & Mason hamper, eating the entire Christmas pudding. Cyril might be a foodie just like his owner, however his cravings have got him into trouble. Rosie comments, 'He doesn't realise what he's eating could be lethal. It's a bit of a design fault.' Design fault indeed, as theobromine and caffeine which are both found in chocolate are incredibly toxic to dogs but they tend to love the taste. As for Cyril's impulsive Christmas pudding snack, dried fruits such as grapes, raisins and currants can cause serious illness in dogs and in the worst scenario, kidney failure. Cats have an acute ability to detect whether a food is nutritious for them, such as high protein wet food, choosing this option over a less nutritional alternative. Meanwhile, dogs do not have this same evolutionary ability, and like children will simply eat whatever food is pleasing to their palate regardless of nutrition or safety. This means mindfulness is key, with owners ensuring potentially lethal foodstuffs are safely out of reach or jumping ability.

Whippets are undoubtedly one of the most loving and sensitive dog breeds. Their complex needs add to their character, with the most important factor being how they are best suited to an individual or family able to spend a large amount of time with their dog – which could be at home relaxing or taking an easy ramble in the countryside as opposed to mountain trekking or long-distance running. Due to relocation to the beautiful southeast seaside town of Deal, eight-year-old Cyril now enjoys a more peaceful life with his family, and though not too fond of the water, he enjoys all the intriguingly new and grotesque smells available to him on his country walks. Rosie is never short of praise for Cyril, with his idiosyncrasies only adding to the tenderness. 'In terms of what he's given us, it's so huge in terms of wellbeing and mental health. There is just an amazing sense of love between us all and he's brought us so much joy.'